# FAMILY

[Left column, partial:]
...dward
...ntagu of
...ks, and of
...ierrepoint,
...aroness
...art of
...ed 1794.

Charles, General, Kt. of the Bath, Governor of Minorca, fought in American War of Independence, born 1753, died 1801. = Louisa, dau. of Lord Vere Bertie, 3rd son of Duke of Ancaster.

William, D.D., Archbishop of Armagh, born 1755, died 1823, leaving issue. = Sophia, dau. of Thomas Penn of Stoke Poges.

*and six daughters:*
Mary, mar. James, 1st Earl of Lonsdale.
Jane, mar. George, Earl Macartney.
Jane, mar. Hugh, 2nd Duke of Northumberland.
Caroline, mar. John, 1st Earl of Portarlington.
Augusta, mar. Captain Andrew Corbet.
Louisa, died unmarried.

...uisa, Lord Lovaine, ...wards ...of Beverley . Duke of ...mberland, had issue: ..., 6th Duke; ...: 3, George; ...enry; ...ed unmarried; ...mar. Edward, Hatherton.

Charles, G.C.B., Ambassador to France, created Lord Stuart de Rothesay, inherited Highcliffe Castle, Hants, born 1779, died 1845. = Elizabeth Margaret Yorke, dau. of Philip, 3rd Earl of Hardwicke died 1867.

John James, R.N. born 1782, died 1811. = Albinia, dau. of Rt. Hon. John Sullivan, had issue, one son, General Charles Stuart.

Charlotte, mar. Charles, Earl Canning, K.G., died at Calcutta, 1861.

Louisa, mar. Henry, 3rd Marquess of Waterford, K.P., died 1891.

...P. for Co. of ...dvocate- ...order of ..., ...neral. = Jane Lawley, dau. of Paul Beilby, 1st Baron Wenlock, died 1900.

Caroline, mar. John Chetwynd Talbot, son of Charles, 2nd Earl Talbot, had issue, John Gilbert, P.C., M.P. for Oxford, Edward, Bishop of Winchester.

Charles Beilby, P.C., K.C., M.P. for Sheffield, born 1851, died 1926, created Baron Stuart of Wortley, mar. 1st. Beatrice, dau. of Thomas Adolphus Trollope, and 2nd, Alice Caroline, dau. of Sir John Millais, Bart., P.R.A.

Mary, mar. Ralph, 2nd Earl of Lovelace.

Margaret, mar. Reginald, son of Henry, 3rd Earl Talbot and 18th Earl of Shrewsbury, Major-General, K.C.B., Governor of Victoria, Australia.

Blanche, mar. Frederick Firebrace, Colonel R.E.

Caroline, mar. Norman de l'Aigle Grosvenor, 3rd son of Robert, 1st Lord Ebury, Gren. Guards, M.P.

Katharine, mar. Neville Lyttelton, 3rd son of George, 4th Lord Lyttelton, General, P.C., Chief of General Staff, Governor of Royal Hospital, Chelsea.

# The Fringes of History

## The Life and Times of Edward Stuart Wortley

Robert Franklin

© Robert Franklin 2003

ISBN 1 897 887 35 3

All rights reserved.
No part of this publication may be reproduced, stored in a retrieval system or transmitted in any form or by any means (electronic, mechanical, photocopying, recording or otherwise) without the prior permission of the copyright holder.

A British Library Cataloguing in Publication data. A catalogue record for this book is available from the British Library.

Printed by: The Cromwell Press Ltd
             Trowbridge, Wiltshire.

Published by: Natula Publications
              5, St Margarets Avenue, Christchurch, BH23 1JD.
              www.natula.co.uk


**Endpapers:**

From: *The First Lady Wharncliffe and Her Family*
by Caroline Grosvenor and Charles Balby, Lord Stuart of Wortley

**Front cover illustration:**

Major Edward Stuart Wortley, KRRC
by Archibald Stuart Wortley
by permission of Highcliffe Sports and Social Club

**Back cover illustrations:**

Highcliffe Castle: the North Tower from the Garden Entrance
Photograph by Dennis Booth, ARPS

'Spy' cartoon of Edward Stuart Wortley, 1899

The amulet given to Edward Stuart Wortley in the Sudan
by permission of the Royal Green Jackets Museum, Winchester

# CONTENTS

| Chapter | | Page |
|---|---|---|
| | *List of Illustrations* | ii |
| | *List of Maps* | iii |
| | *List of Genealogical Tables* | iii |
| | Preface | iv |
| One | Background and Early Life | 1 |
| Two | Afghanistan | 7 |
| Three | Egypt and the Sudan (1) | 14 |
| Four | Egypt and the Sudan (2) | 25 |
| Five | Marriage and the Army | 33 |
| Six | Egypt and the Sudan (3) | 41 |
| Seven | The Boer War (1) | 50 |
| Eight | The Boer War (2) – The Gordon Relief Expedition | 64 |
| Nine | Home from the Boer War | 70 |
| Ten | Paris and the Entente Cordiale | 75 |
| Eleven | Half Pay | 82 |
| Twelve | The Kaiser at Highcliffe | 86 |
| Thirteen | The *Daily Telegraph* 'Interview' | 92 |
| Fourteen | Shorncliffe | 100 |
| Fifteen | The Great War (1) | 105 |
| Sixteen | The Great War (2) – The First Day of The Somme | 117 |
| Seventeen | Ireland | 125 |
| Eighteen | The Family in Wartime | 130 |
| Nineteen | Retirement (1) | 134 |
| Twenty | Retirement (2) | 140 |
| | *Bibliography* | 145 |
| | *References* | 151 |
| | *Index* | 163 |

# ILLUSTRATIONS

|  | Page |
|---|---|
| 'Eddie' by 'Spy' | 3 |
| Wortley Hall | 5 |
| General Sir Garnet Wolseley | 15 |
| The Battle of Tel-el-Kebir | 17 |
| General Sir Evelyn Wood VC | 19 |
| General Charles Gordon | 21 |
| Col. Sir Hebert Stewart's column crossing the desert | 28 |
| The Battle of Abu Klea | 30 |
| Louisa, Marchioness of Waterford | 34 |
| Highcliffe Castle | 36 |
| Edward Montagu-Stuart-Wortley-Mackenzie | 38 |
| Major Edward Stuart Wortley | 42 |
| Gunboat *Melik* | 44 |
| The Charge of the 21$^{st}$ Lancers at Omdurman | 46 |
| General Sir Redvers Buller VC | 53 |
| Watching the Battle of Colenso | 55 |
| Winston Churchill in 1899 | 57 |
| General Sir Frederick Roberts VC | 59 |
| British soldiers at Tugela Heights | 61 |
| General Sir Herbert Kitchener | 65 |
| The Prince of Wales and The Hon. John Scott Montagu | 73 |
| King Edward VII in 1904 | 76 |
| The Marquis de Soveral | 78 |
| Kaiser Willhelm II | 87 |
| The Kaiser and his entourage at Highcliffe Castle | 89 |
| Major-General Edward Stuart Wortley | 104 |

# ILLUSTRATIONS (II)

|  | Page |
|---|---|
| Field Marshal Sir John French | 108 |
| The Hohenzollern Redoubt | 110 |
| General Sir Douglas Haig in 1916 | 114 |
| Captain Reginald Young on 1$^{st}$ July, 1916 | 118 |
| British troops in a support trench, 1916 | 121 |
| The Territorials at Pozieres, 1916 | 123 |
| Queen Mary at Highcliffe Castle | 137 |
| Violet Stuart Wortley | 141 |

# MAPS

| | |
|---|---|
| Sudan | 26 |
| South Africa | 51 |
| The Western Front, 1916 | 106 |
| The British Zone of the Western Front, 1916 | 112 |
| The Somme Front, 1916 | 116 |

# GENEALOGICAL TABLES

| | |
|---|---|
| The Stuart Wortley Family | Endpapers |
| Edward Stuart Wortley | vi |

# PREFACE

THE STORY of General Stuart Wortley has been told in *The Stuarts of Highcliffe*: it deserves to be told in greater detail; and it can now be told more fully, in the light of material released at the Public Record Office. A War Office file of papers to do with the circumstances of Eddy's departure from the Western Front in 1916 was to have been closed for a hundred years, but it was opened in 1998, with other personal files, on the instructions of the Lord Chancellor.

The late Earl of Wharncliffe's Trustees have allowed me to quote from the Wharncliffe Muniments, Sheffield Archives; the Trustees of the Liddell Hart Centre for Military Archives, King's College, London, have allowed me to quote from the Lyttelton Papers; and the Keeper of Archives and Special Collections, The University Library, University of Durham, has given me permission to make use of the Wingate Papers.

I was given permission at the Bodleian Library to quote from *Papers Concerning the Daily Telegraph Incident*, but the question of copyright in the Kaiser's letters arose, and one of the staff of the German Historical Institute in London was good enough to obtain for me the opinion that no additional consent was necessary. Most of my quotations are brief and have not required special permission; excerpts from *England 1870-1914*, by Sir Robert Ensor, and *A New History of Ireland*, edited by W.E. Vaughan, are reprinted by permission of Oxford University Press.

I want to thank Barbara Mackay for showing me the diaries kept by her father, Roger Dixey, during the Great War, and for letting me print his laconic entry for $1^{st}$ July 1916. I also want to thank Martin Middlebrook for his generosity in giving me the use of maps from his invaluable book *The First Day on the Somme*. The other maps I have used come from *Sir Garnet Wolseley*, by Halik Kochanski, by courtesy of the publishers, the Hambledon Press.

I am grateful for the help of the staffs of many archives, libraries, museums, and other bodies: Beaulieu Photographic Library; the Bodleian Library; the British Library, the Courtauld Institute; Durham University Library; Eton College Archives; Folkestone and Sandgate Libraries; Hampshire Record Office; Highcliffe Sports and Social Club; the Historical Manuscripts Commission; the Imperial War Museum; the Liddell Hart Centre for Military Archives; the National Army Museum; the National Maritime Museum; the National Portrait Gallery; the Public Record Office; the Regimental Museum of the Royal Green Jackets; Sheffield Leisure Services; and Southampton University Library.

Much advice and help has come from Mike Allen and Ian Stevenson, whose combined knowledge of Highcliffe and the Castle is second to none. Peter Elwes, Maud Frampton and Pip Hatton kindly shared with me their memories of Eddy and his family. Lastly, I want to record here the fact that Peter Elwes presented the portrait of Violet Stuart Wortley by his father Simon Elwes RA to the Hampshire County Council Museums Service in 2002, with the intention that it should be returned to Christchurch: the portrait now hangs in the Red House Museum, Christchurch.

This book has been produced with assistance from the Red House Museum, Christchurch, Archives and Local History Fund.

Highcliffe, 2003                          Robert Franklin

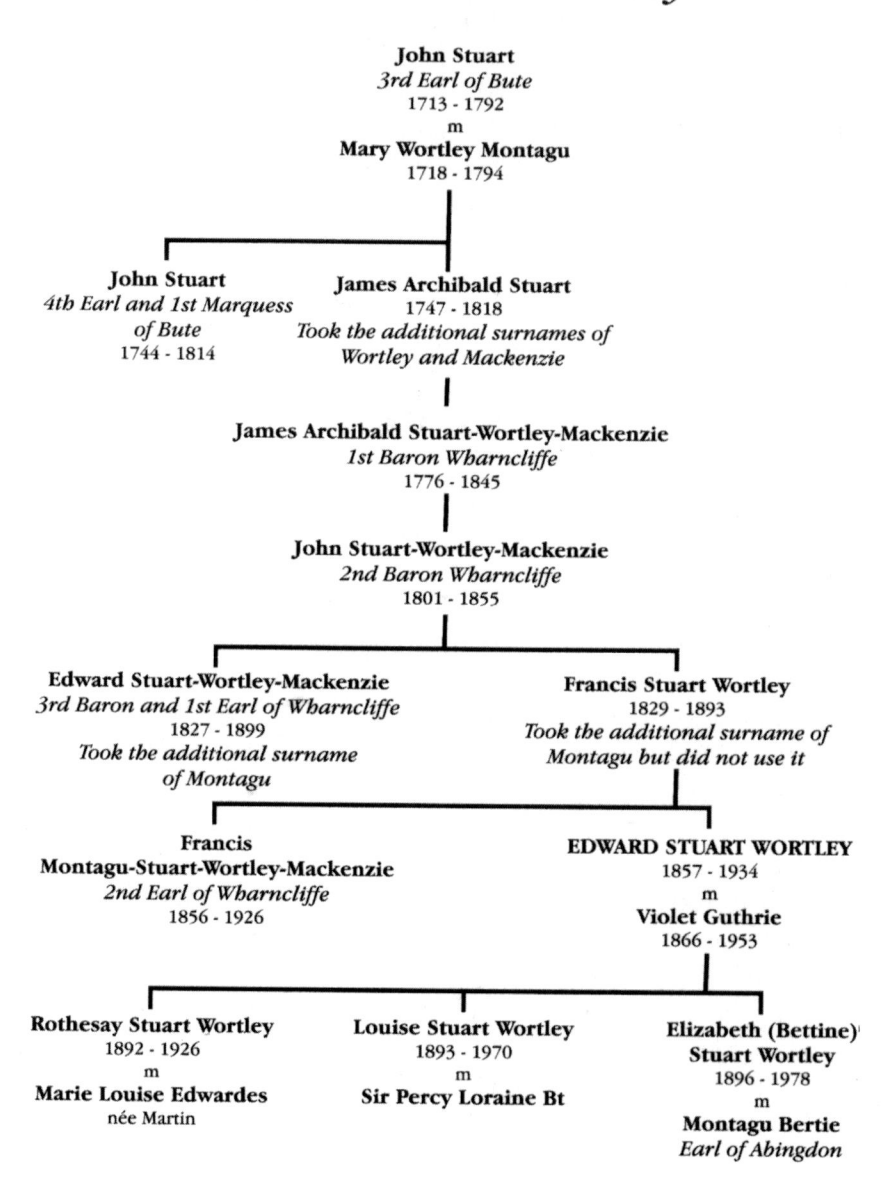

# *Edward Stuart Wortley*

**John Stuart**
*3rd Earl of Bute*
1713 - 1792
m
**Mary Wortley Montagu**
1718 - 1794

**John Stuart**
*4th Earl and 1st Marquess
of Bute*
1744 - 1814

**James Archibald Stuart**
1747 - 1818
*Took the additional surnames of
Wortley and Mackenzie*

**James Archibald Stuart-Wortley-Mackenzie**
*1st Baron Wharncliffe*
1776 - 1845

**John Stuart-Wortley-Mackenzie**
*2nd Baron Wharncliffe*
1801 - 1855

**Edward Stuart-Wortley-Mackenzie**
*3rd Baron and 1st Earl of Wharncliffe*
1827 - 1899
*Took the additional surname
of Montagu*

**Francis Stuart Wortley**
1829 - 1893
*Took the additional surname of
Montagu but did not use it*

**Francis
Montagu-Stuart-Wortley-Mackenzie**
*2nd Earl of Wharncliffe*
1856 - 1926

**EDWARD STUART WORTLEY**
1857 - 1934
m
**Violet Guthrie**
1866 - 1953

**Rothesay Stuart Wortley**
1892 - 1926
m
**Marie Louise Edwardes**
née Martin

**Louise Stuart Wortley**
1893 - 1970
m
**Sir Percy Loraine Bt**

**Elizabeth (Bettine)
Stuart Wortley**
1896 - 1978
m
**Montagu Bertie**
*Earl of Abingdon*

# CHAPTER ONE

## BACKGROUND AND EARLY LIFE

EDWARD JAMES MONTAGU STUART WORTLEY was always known as Eddy; and that name conjured up for his generation the figure that 'Spy' made of him in *Vanity Fair*, on 26$^{th}$ October, 1899: tall, slim, handsome and debonair; a 'darling of the gods'. Later generations have sensed that his life was a disappointment to him in some respects: privately, there was the death of his only son; all too publicly, there was the collapse of his career.

In retrospect, his career is most interesting for his activities on the fringes of history: the small but significant parts that he played in the Gordon Relief Expedition, the Battle of Omdurman and the Entente Cordiale; his attempt to improve Anglo-German relations, through his acquaintance with the Kaiser; and the events of the first day of the Battle of the Somme. Of these, however, only Omdurman and the Entente Cordiale can have given him much satisfaction.

Eddy was born to privilege. He was descended from John Stuart, 3$^{rd}$ Earl of Bute, and Mary, Countess of Bute. The Earl, himself descended, though illegitimately, from Scottish kings, was George III's favourite for some time and briefly his Prime Minister. The Countess was the daughter of Lady Mary Wortley Montagu, whose husband, Edward Wortley Montagu, comes into the story not only as the Countess's father but also as a rich man with estates in Yorkshire and Cornwall. Edward Wortley Montagu disapproved of his only son and disinherited him; his property passed first to Lady Mary and then to the Countess. This property included Wharncliffe Chase, with Wharncliffe Lodge and Wortley Hall, on Yorkshire's border with Derbyshire, near Sheffield.

The 3$^{rd}$ Earl of Bute's eldest son, John Stuart, Lord Mountstuart, inherited the earldom of Bute and the property that went with it; and, later, as 4$^{th}$ Earl, he was given a step in the peerage to become the 1st Marquess of Bute. It was the 3rd Earl's second son, James Archibald Stuart, who inherited from the Countess the property that had come to her from her father. James Archibald also inherited estates in Scotland, from his uncle, his father's younger brother, James Stuart Mackenzie, Lord Privy Seal of Scotland. The additional surname of Mackenzie was adopted by this James when he himself inherited the estates that had come to the family from Sir George Mackenzie of Rosehaugh, Lord Advocate of Scotland, whose daughter married the 1st Earl of Bute.

James Archibald Stuart adopted the additional surnames of Wortley and Mackenzie. He was a scapegrace as a young man, but he began to take life seriously as an MP and, in due course, as a great landowner, 'he settled down a model landlord'.[1] He married Margaret, daughter of Sir David Cuninghame, Bart. His son, also James Archibald, was a statesman, raised to the peerage as 1st Baron Wharncliffe; by this time, he had married Lady Caroline Creighton, daughter of the 1st Earl of Erne, and his father had handed over to him the Wharncliffe estate. He is best known to history as one of the 'Waverers' in the Reform Bill crisis of 1832, but he is remembered, too, as Lord Privy Seal and Lord President of the Council under Sir Robert Peel.

James Archibald Stuart-Wortley-Mackenzie the younger, 1st Baron Wharncliffe, was succeeded as 2nd Baron by his son, John, Eddy's grandfather. He married Lady Georgiana Ryder, daughter of the 1st Earl of Harrowby, and they lived a more or less private life. He was succeeded as 3rd Baron by his eldest son, Edward, who was later given two steps in the peerage, to become 1st Earl of Wharncliffe, and took the further surname of Montagu. He married Lady Susan Lascelles, daughter of the 3rd Earl of Harewood; they had no children and his heir was his brother, Francis, Eddy's father. Francis, too, took the additional surname of Montagu, but he and his family used the simple form of the patronymic, Stuart Wortley, without a hyphen.

**'Eddie' by 'Spy'**

One of the series of cartoons called 'Men of the Day' drawn for *Vanity Fair* by 'Spy' (Sir Leslie Ward). It was published 26th October, 1899.

Francis was called to the Bar by the Inner Temple and practiced as a barrister. He married Maria Elizabeth Martin, daughter of William Bennet Martin of Worsborough Hall, near Barnsley, and there were seven children, of whom only five survived into adult life: Francis John; Edward James; Ralph Granville; Alan Richard, known as Richard; and Mary Susan. They lived for many years at Scarborough, a place that Francis regarded as his home. 'I am fond of the place,' he wrote, in a sad letter to his brother, Edward, the Earl of Wharncliffe, in middle age, when alcoholism seemed likely to destroy his life, 'have formed for myself much and useful occupation, and, though I daresay you hardly believe it, am respected and looked up to, even by bitter political opponents, who have no regard for rank or position.'[2]

Eddy was born on 31st July, 1857, at 25 South Street, Grosvenor Square;[3] he spent his early childhood at Scarborough. He started at Eton in April 1866, at the age of eight, but he left the school in December 1870, when he was thirteen,[4] and the likelihood is that he was withdrawn because his father could no longer pay the fees: only two years later, Francis had to ask Edward to help pay his tradesmen's bills.[5] Scarcely any records of his teenage years have come to light, but he was probably sent to live for some time with his father's sister, Mary, in Ireland. Mary had married Henry, 3rd Marquess of Drogheda and their home was Moore Abbey, at Monasterevin, in County Kildare. He wrote to his mother enthusiastically about Ireland and familiarly about Moore Abbey, later, when he heard that she was to pay the Droghedas a visit.[6] He began his military career by joining the Kildare Rifles, a militia regiment, on 9th February, 1876, at the age of nineteen.[7]

It is clear that the consequences of Francis's alcoholism obliged other members of the family to take over his duties as a parent. Edward, Earl of Wharncliffe, was in some respects a surrogate father; as has been said, he had no children of his own, and in the natural course of events the earldom and what went with it would have passed first to Francis and then to his eldest son, also Francis but known as Frank, Eddy's brother. As it happened, Francis did not

**Wortley Hall, Sheffield**

Photograph by courtesy of Sheffield Newspapers Limited

live to inherit and it was Frank who succeeded. Thus Eddy and his brothers and sister were made welcome at Wortley and at Wharncliffe House, in Curzon Street, by the Earl, their uncle, and the Countess, their aunt. They must have known both houses well.

The piece that accompanied Spy's cartoon of Eddy in *Vanity Fair* suggested that he failed the entrance examination to Sandhurst and used the militia as a back door into the regular army.[8] This is an example of what has been called 'the pointed mischief of a *Vanity Fair* profile'.[9] Whether or not Eddy failed the examination, it is true that many men who did so joined the militia and then transferred to the regular army; it is also true that the militia had its own examinations, and that it provided the regular army with most of its officers at this time.[10] The writer might have made more mischief out of the fact that the Commandant of the Kildare Rifles was Eddy's uncle, the Marquess of Drogheda.

# CHAPTER TWO

## AFGHANISTAN

EDDY WAS COMMISSIONED into the King's Royal Rifle Corps on 13$^{th}$ October, 1877,[1] and he joined the 4$^{th}$ Battalion of the regiment at Agra, in India, in January 1878.[2] It was the heyday of the Raj, and perhaps young officers never lived as well as Eddy and his friends did in India then. He and four other subalterns, who shared a bungalow, had at their beck and call a number of servants 'about equal', he estimated, 'to a home battalion on a peace footing'.[3] They had their duties, but these left much of their time for sport, particularly polo, the sport of princes if not of kings. 'In those days,' Eddy wrote, 'the price of polo ponies was within the means of even junior officers.'[4]

His letters show that he was still at Agra in November 1878, when the Second Afghan War began. Britain and Russia had been vying for influence over Afghanistan, in the 'Great Game', since the beginning of the nineteenth century, and Britain had asserted herself with disastrous results in the First Afghan War of 1838-1842. In 1878 the Amir of Afghanistan, Shir Ali, received a Russian mission at Kabul but had a British mission turned back at the frontier. British protests and an ultimatum were ignored, and Afghanistan was invaded by three armies: Shir Ali's forces were overwhelmed and he himself fled the country and died soon afterwards. In May 1879, the new Amir, Shir Ali's son, Yakub Khan, had no option but to accept British terms for peace, set out in the Treaty of Gandamak.

The Treaty of Gandamak provided for the establishment of a British mission at Kabul, which was led by Sir Louis Cavagnari. In September 1879, Sir Louis and his entire staff were butchered by Afghan soldiers, said to be mutinous and out of control, and the war began again. Of the three armies that had invaded Afghanistan, the Kurram Force, garrisoning a fort in the Kurram Valley, seventy miles from Kabul, was best placed to strike again. This force was commanded by General Sir Frederick Roberts, who was at Simla when the news of the massacre was brought to him. Eddy was based in the north by this time. 'I was at Mussoorie when the dreadful news of the Kabul massacre arrived', he wrote to his mother, 'and anticipating an immediate advance I telegraphed to Simla and offered my services either as transport officer or signaller. To my great delight, I was ordered immediately to the Kurram Valley.'[5]

The next letter in the series that we have came from Rawalpindi, about two-thirds of the way from Mussoorie to the Kurram Valley. Eddy's way ahead lay through Kohat and Thal, but he expected to have to make a detour through Peshawar in order to obtain transport, and between Peshawar and Kohat there was a certain pass in the hills at which he would be at risk of ambush by local tribesman: he would need an escort here. He told his mother that he had been assembling his kit for Afghanistan, which was not to weigh more than eighty pounds, apart from a shared tent. Another item that was not included in the allowance was his dog. 'Tyke the warrior is here and has been equipped for service – and is under orders for the front,' he wrote. 'I am thinking of sharpening his teeth.'[6]

By the time that Eddy arrived at the Kurram, Roberts had arrived and departed again, moving forward with the main body of his force towards Kushi, where he made the final preparations for his descent on Kabul. He left Kushi on 30th September and entered Kabul on 10th October, having fought what was later described as 'a critical action' on his way.[7] Perhaps it would have been possible for Eddy to catch up with Roberts, but he explained to his mother that he had not been given the chance to do so. 'I was not fortunate enough to get into the advance as I am a junior officer in the Transport Department: and there was no signalling appointment vacant,' he wrote.[8] Left behind, he announced that he was appointed Superintendent of Field Transport at base: he was responsible for 'all the animals such as camels, mules, elephants and bullocks belonging to the Kurram Valley Field Force'.[9]

'The work is very hard:' he told his mother, 'and I am in my office from 7 a.m. to 6 p.m. I have to see all the animals fed twice a day and to supply food for them.'[10] He also had to see that the men who worked with the animals received their rations. It was not easy to make sure of obtaining food for the animals, and it made matters worse in this respect that he never knew from one day to the next how many animals would have to be fed. Several years later, when he must have thought all this was behind him, he received a letter informing him that his paperwork of the time had not been properly completed, and that an amount of twenty-seven thousand pounds was unaccounted for. A futile correspondence ensued until Eddy, knowing full well that his account was overdrawn, sent the official concerned a cheque for the full amount, with a note wishing him luck.[11] He heard no more.

Though Kabul was in British hands, Afghanistan was not by any means reconciled to British hegemony. Indeed, some tribes recognized no authority. The Kurram Valley was part of the fiefdom of a particularly lawless tribe called the Zaimukhts, which kept clear of it while the garrison was at full strength but returned as soon as Roberts' force marched out. On 30th September a marauding band murdered a British officer, and General Thomas Gordon, who had succeeded Roberts in command, requested and obtained permission from the Indian Government to mount a punitive expedition against the tribe.[12] Other matters took precedence, but in a letter on 26th October Eddy told his mother that plans for the expedition were being drawn up, and that he hoped to be able to join it.[13] This letter ends with the news that he had grown a beard but shaved it off because it made him feel 'such a beast.'

Eddy joined the punitive expedition against the Zaimukhts as a signals officer. One record has it that he was 'Superintendent and Assistant Superintendent of Army Signalling, Kurram Force',[14] from 1st December, though why the appointments were given in this way is not explained. Brigadier-General John Tytler, VC, was given command of the expedition, and he marshalled his forces at a place called Balesh Khel. This, Eddy wrote, is 'barren land on a small hill and situated at the entrance of the pass which leads from the Kurram Valley to the Zaimukht Valley'. 'The pass', he added, 'is very dangerous: and has to be watched ...'[15] The expedition set out from Balesh Khel on 8th December, to cross Zaimukht territory to the Zaimukht stronghold of Zawo, and at first it was unopposed, as it levied fines and burned down the homes of those who would not pay.

Zawo is described in the official history of the war as 'a regular mountain fastness:'[16] it could only be approached through a narrow gorge or along rough tracks over the hills on each side. General Tytler's plan was to lead the main body of his force through the gorge while two columns of men, one on each side, made their way along the tracks above him to protect his flanks, and Eddy was attached to the right hand column, commanded by Colonel John Gordon. On 12th December, Eddy observed, ahead of his column, 'a collection of some two thousand men waving their swords in the air and dancing eccentric war dances'.[17] His first responsibility was to send a heliogram with this information to General Tytler, but then he found himself in action and under fire for the first time.[18]

The official history notes that the enemy was first found in a particularly strong position.[19] Eddy described it as 'to all appearances impregnable'.[20] 'A direct attack having failed,' the official history goes on, 'the position was turned, but even then the enemy did not retire until turned out by a sharp hand-to-hand encounter.'[21] During the days that followed, Colonel Gordon's column gradually pushed the Zaimukhts back through hilly and mountainous terrain, until those who could took refuge in Zawo or slipped away to their own villages. Meanwhile, General Tytler and his men had fought their way through the gorge; in their final approach to Zawo they were obliged to proceed 'in single file under a heavy fire and shower of rocks from the heights on the left',[22] but the stronghold soon fell to them.

Weapons and fortifications were destroyed, and more fines were levied and houses burned down. Then the entire force withdrew;

and the official account has it that it did so unmolested, 'for which the reason appears to be that the enemy had, in their hand-to-hand encounters with the right column, lost heavily'.[23] British casualties were two killed and two wounded. Later, perhaps not surprisingly, Eddy felt a sense of anti-climax: in an account of the action that seems to have been intended to be enclosed with a letter, he said he supposed he would have to revert to his transport role, but would prefer either to go to Kabul or to rejoin his regiment in India.[24] He had had a bout of fever, and this may have had a depressing effect. He must have been cheered, however, when he knew that he had been mentioned in despatches.

He did have to revert to his transport role, and he did not like it. 'I hold a very fair appointment....,' he wrote to his mother from the Kurram in the spring of 1880, 'but then I want to see fighting – and hate office work; with all the official unpleasantry (sic) and accounts I have to get through.'[25] He repeated his preference for a return to regimental duties, but he did not mention Kabul, where Roberts was struggling with both military and political problems. A little later, his situation had changed for the better, if only temporarily. He was in a camp in a beautiful part of the country, not clearly identifiable from his letter but evidently not far from his base, which reminded him of England; and he was looking forward to three days of hunting in the hills with a friend. 'I am going right up into the snows to try for a bear:' he wrote, 'it will be very jolly up there.'[26]

By the summer of 1880 much had changed for Britain in Afghanistan: in brief, it had become clear that Britain could not control Afghanistan, much less extend to that country the rule that was established in India. Yakub Khan had abdicated and his cousin, Abdurrahman Khan, had been recognized as Amir, but Yakub's younger brother, Ayub Khan, had challenged his authority. It had already been decided that the north of Afghanistan should be left to Abdurrahman when Ayub inflicted a humiliating defeat on a British force at Maiwand, and besieged what was left of it in Kandahar. British prestige was restored by Roberts' spectacular march to the rescue, from Kabul to Kandahar, and his complete victory over Ayub: but after that it was decided that the south of the country, too, should be left to the Amir. British forces were evacuated and Abdurrahman ruled, under British protection, until his death in 1901.

That summer, Eddy was sent to Simla on sick leave. The only clue that we have to the reason is provided by a letter to his mother, dated 22$^{nd}$ August, 1880:[27] 'My arm is better, but has to be cut again at Simla after which it will, I hope get well, but at present it is quite useless to me.' This suggests that the problem was some infected lesion, perhaps a wound. He had much to say in this letter about the disaster at Maiwand and the outcome of the war; Maiwand was, for him, 'the most disgraceful defeat that British arms have ever suffered'; by the war, in his view, Britain had 'absolutely gained nothing'. He was in a low mood again. He had been told that he would be on sick leave for three months and he was not looking forward to it. 'I really cannot afford to kick my heels at Simla for three months,' he wrote gloomily.

Then, in January 1881, he was sent from India to South Africa with the 2$^{nd}$ Battalion of his regiment, which was to reinforce the British army struggling against the Boers of the Transvaal:[28] they were too late. Britain had annexed the Boer republic of the Transvaal in 1877, on the grounds that it was in a state of anarchy that might spread to the other white communities in South Africa, the Orange Free State, Natal and Cape Colony. The British Government would not commit itself either to a return to independence or to the alternative of self-government, and in 1880 the Boers rose in revolt. Military reverses and – ironically – the risk of the spread of unrest persuaded the Cabinet to negotiate; and the Transvaal was returned to the Boers, under British suzerainty, in 1881.

Given leave in South Africa, Eddy and a friend decided on an expedition across the country in a two-wheeled vehicle called an American spider carriage, with four ponies: the journey was to take them from Natal into the Orange Free State and then into Cape

Colony; their destination was Kimberley. At Bloemfontein, on their way, they were offered a tract of land in the Transvaal in exchange for the carriage and ponies. They knew they would be able to sell the ponies well at Kimberley, and they preferred cash in hand to a stretch of veldt they had never seen. 'So we drove to Kimberley,' Eddy recalled. 'Here we certainly realized a good sum for the ponies, but later discovered that the 20,000 acres on offer comprised the whole of what was to be the Witwatersrand mines.'[29] These were gold mines.

# CHAPTER THREE

## EGYPT AND THE SUDAN (1)

AN IMPORTANT CHAPTER in the story of Eddy's life and career opened in 1882, when a British expeditionary force was sent to Egypt, and he with it. Egypt was part of the Ottoman Empire, ruled by the Sultan's viceroy, the Khedive, who had allowed the country to sink so deeply into debt to the European Powers that he had had to hand over his country's finances to European emissaries. Nationalist feeling, always running high on account of Turkish suzerainty, had finally overflowed at this, and the army had seized power. The stakes were thus raised for the European Powers, Britain being threatened with loss of control of the Suez Canal, and armed intervention was considered necessary. Because the other European Powers were unwilling allies, and Turkey was an unreliable ally, Britain acted alone.

Eddy's wife, in one of her volumes of autobiography, has it that Eddy was sent to Egypt as a sort of exile, at the behest of a certain duchess.[1] According to this story, Her Grace had encouraged him in his attentions to her daughter in the belief that he was the Earl of Wharncliffe's heir, and was horrified when she discovered her mistake. This may be so, but in the records there is a letter from Eddy to Lord Wharncliffe, dated 10$^{th}$ August, 1886, four years later, in which almost the same story appears, in more detail.[2] Eddy told his uncle that the duchess and her connections had wanted to have him sent to India, but that his friends' influence at the War Office had proved stronger than theirs; it was a storm in a teacup, in any case, he added, since he had promised not to see the girl again.

The commander of the expeditionary force was General Sir Garnet Wolseley, who landed at Ismailia on 21$^{st}$ August, 1882, and made sure of the Suez Canal before turning his attention to Cairo. One of the obstacles in his way was the Egyptian base at Tel-el-Kebir, and here the one great battle of this brief campaign took place, on 13$^{th}$

**General Sir Garnet Wolseley**
Later Field Marshal The Viscount Wolseley
By Paul Albert Besnard
By courtesy of the National Portrait Gallery, London.

September. The lack of cover in the open desert and the fierce heat of the sun persuaded him to make his approach by night and his attack at dawn, a plan that worried his staff but was completely successful: the British force was in position when the order came, and the Egyptians were taken by surprise. 'Several thousand men moved as quietly as though they only numbered ten', Eddy recalled.[3]

Eddy was ADC to General Baker Russell, a cavalry officer, whose job, under General Drury Lowe, was to cut off the retreat of as many of the enemy as possible and to pursue the rest to Cairo. The story of the pursuit and the capitulation of the entire Egyptian Army gained the status of legend, but though Eddy spoke of it later he did not speak of his own part in it.[4] He was present at the battle;[5] otherwise, the most that can be said is that he probably rode with General Russell when the cavalry chased the routed Egyptians across the desert, and that he was probably present when General Lowe received the surrender of the Egyptian Army and the Egyptian capital. There was no further fighting after Tel-el Kebir: 'ten thousand Egyptian troops surrendered their weapons without resistance'.[6]

The British expeditionary forces restored order and restored legitimate authority in the person of the Khedive, but it was unable to withdraw having done so: what it could not do was restore good government; and the Khedive could not do so either, because his authority was not backed by a police force or an army. Thus the objects for which the campaign had been fought were saved but not safe. It has been said that the rest of the world was prepared for Britain to annex Egypt and the Sudan after Tel-el-Kebir[7], but the British Government was unwilling to go so far. Instead there was a fudge: Sir Evelyn Baring was sent out ostensibly as British representative but actually as British governor, with the title of Agent and Consul-General.

An immediate task for the new Egyptian administration, under British auspices, was the creation of a new army, which was to have

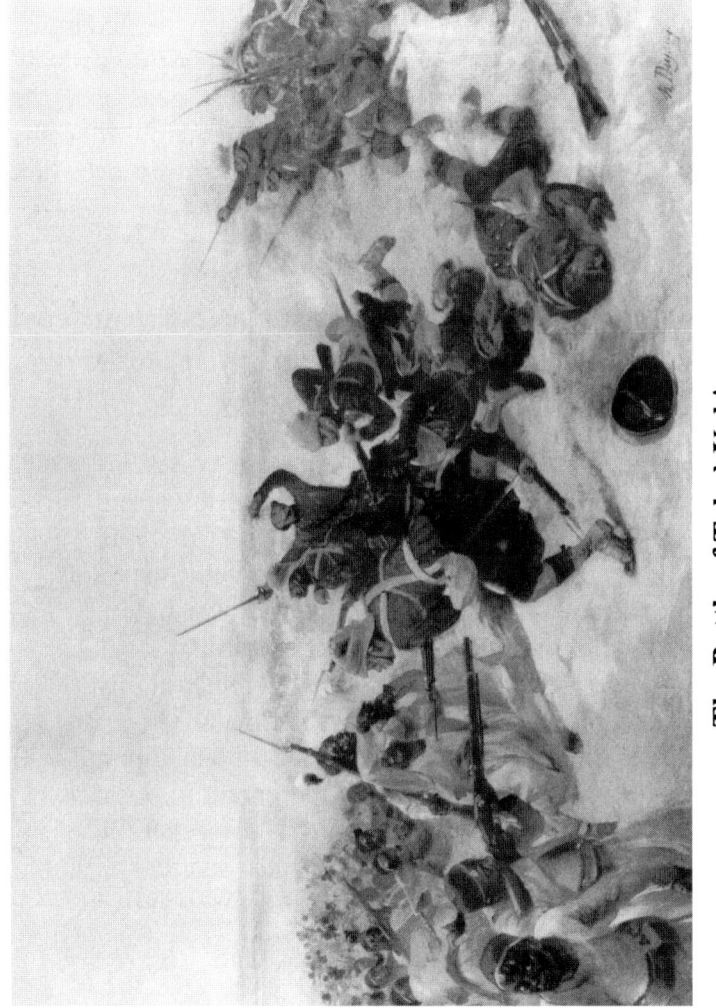

**The Battle of Tel-el-Kebir**
The Black Watch leading The Highland Brigade
By Henri Louis Dupray
By courtesy of the Director, National Army Museum, London.

British officers. Eddy is said to have been 'the first active British officer to enter the Egyptian service after 1882',[8] and early in 1883 he was appointed ADC to the Sirdar or Commander-in-Chief of the Egyptian Army, General Sir Evelyn Wood, VC.[9] At the end of 1882, however, he was briefly Military Secretary to Valentine Baker.[10] This officer was dismissed from the British Army in 1875 as the result of a scandal, but he rose to the rank of general in the Turkish Army and then transferred to the Egyptian Army. It seems to be the case that when the British authorities caught up with him again in 1882 they relegated him to the Egyptian police, with the rank of colonel.[11]

There are several letters in the records from the Sirdar to Lord Wharncliffe in which Eddy is mentioned; one of them, dated 6th May, 1883 is worth quoting at length.

> I cannot understand your nephew – perhaps you or his Aunt Susan said something to him, or possibly I did and have forgotten it, but he is working if anything too hard. He has Arabic lessons six or seven times a week and German three or four. I didn't know before he could put his shoulder so well into the collar. He is really a very good fellow and takes most kindly anything I say to him. Not that I have said anything of late for I have had absolutely no occasion. I take him to the office for the whole of every forenoon in order to initiate him into staff work, and I am generally trying to pass into his hands the military secretary's work. The fault I feared in his character – want of earnestness, if it existed will I hope pass away.[12]

He added that Baker Russell, now Sir Baker, had recently spoken to him 'in high terms' of Eddy.

The Sirdar returned to England for two months in the summer of 1883. Eddy, who came with him, had leave, and his letters to Lord Wharncliffe provide a glimpse of his family life and social life at

**General Sir Evelyn Wood VC**
By an unknown artist
By courtesy of the Director, National Army Museum, London.

that time.[13] There are references to his father's alcoholism and his mother's misery on account of it, his debts and his relationship with an Irish girl, Constance Vesey, of whom the family disapproved. Lord Wharncliffe evidently grumbled about his debts but always paid up, perhaps, as Eddy slyly remarked on one occasion, because he liked to see his nephew cutting a dash. His relationship with Miss Vesey was another matter, however: it was made clear that an allowance that Lord Wharncliffe made him would cease if he married her; and it went without saying that his father could not do much for him.

A year later, at the beginning of 1884, Eddy met General Gordon. The Egyptian Sudan had been in a state of insurrection since 1881, under the leadership of a fanatical religious figure, known as the Mahdi. Attempts to pacify the country had failed, sometimes disastrously, and the governments in Cairo and London had agreed that it was no longer governable; it was to be left to the Sudanese. The Egyptian garrisons, which included soldiers and civilians, men, women and children, had first to be withdrawn, however, and they would have to travel long distances through hostile territory. It would be a difficult and dangerous operation, and Gordon, a previous Governor-General of the Sudan, had been put in charge of it.

Charles George Gordon's fame now rests chiefly on the circumstances of his death at Khartoum in 1885, but he was an admired and respected figure in his own generation. He was a highly successful military engineer and commander of irregular forces in China, and an equally successful administrator in Central Africa and the Sudan. He was also a devoutly religious man. Independence of mind and some idiosyncrasy of thought and behaviour, which were characteristic of him, made for difficulties in relationships between him and the military and political authorities of his day: and a less easily definable characteristic, perhaps most easily understood in terms of his religious beliefs, compounded these difficulties: there was something messianic about him.

**General Charles Gordon**
By Julia Abercrombie
By courtesy of the National Portrait Gallery, London.

Gordon spent two days in Cairo in January 1884, when his instructions were amended. He was to be the Governor-General of the Sudan again, until such time as he was able not only to evacuate the Egyptian garrisons but also to set up a Sudanese administration. He stayed with the Sirdar: 'Gordon stayed with Sir Evelyn in Cairo,' Eddy's wife quoted him as having said 'and I had the privilege of seeing a good deal of this remarkable character during the course of his visit.'[14] On the evening of his departure, Lady Wood gave a dinner for him; and then Sir Evelyn drove him to the railway station, where a party of well-wishers waited to say goodbye to him. Whether or not Eddy was at the dinner, as Sir Evelyn's ADC, he was one of the party at the station.[15]

Having established himself at Khartoum, Gordon began the evacuation of the Egyptian garrisons and made plans for a Sudanese administration. The man whom he proposed should lead the administration, a Sudanese Arab with the qualities that he believed necessary but an unsavoury past, was not acceptable to the British Government; and in the Cabinet there ensued a dangerously desultory discussion of this issue in particular and Gordon's mission in general. The Mahdi was more active, and before long Khartoum was under siege and more or less cut off from the outside world. Then the question that exercised the minds of the members of the Cabinet, at first only intermittently, was whether or not it was necessary to mount a relief expedition.

Meanwhile, the Mahdi's influence was spreading north, and steps had to be taken to counter any attempt that he might make to invade Egypt. Eddy was restless, and the Sirdar gave him command of a force of five hundred Arab irregulars, with instructions to patrol one of the possible invasion routes in the Western Desert; he was also to set up bases at two strategic points, the Great Oasis, in Egypt, and the oasis of Selimeh (Selima) in the Sudan.[16] Accompanying him as the only other British officer and Englishman was Henry Colvile, who was to act independently and report on the state of the roads that they travelled.[17] Colvile later wrote the official history of the Sudan Campaign.

First, however, he had to transform a motley collection of men, whose language he had barely mastered, into a quasi-military unit: he had also to ensure that the men and their transport animals, horses and camels, were provided with all that they would need on their expedition into the desert; everything including food and water for men and animals, would have to be carried. It was interesting and instructive work, he explained to his mother, in a letter dated 21$^{st}$ May, 1884,[18] the tone of which was no doubt set to reassure her. ' I took 60 of my savages out for a gallop on Monday, and laughed a great deal,' he wrote. 'They sing all the time, or rather utter curious weird cries, and when they charge their arms and legs fly in the air and they go helter-skelter in a very loose formation.'

But even in this letter there was a note of unease: he had no second-in-command to support him, and he was going into relatively unknown country. And in a letter to his friend and fellow ADC Reginald Wingate, two days earlier, he had been distinctly downbeat.[19] He was worried about provisions and transport, but he could not obtain the help or advice that he felt he needed; and, what was more, his men were unarmed. 'We are therefore, I suppose, to fight with our fists', he remarked bitterly. He was then at Assioutt (Asyut), south of Cairo, and he had sent a telegram to the Sirdar, asking for further instructions, but a reply had come from Herbert Kitchener, his immediate superior for the time being, ordering him not to go over his head.

A more helpful reply came from Wingate:[20] he had explained Eddy's position to the Sirdar diplomatically, and Sir Evelyn had instructed him to ensure that Kitchener understood it; he agreed that Eddy had not been treated as well as he might have been, but urged him not to overreact. Reminding him gently of the Commander-in-Chief's responsibilities, he suggested that it was not unreasonable to expect him to act through Kitchener. Finally, with soldierly sangfroid, he wished his friend 'a pleasant journey'. Tactful as Wingate was, however, he implied some criticism of Kitchener, who had apparently failed so far to keep the Sirdar as well informed about Eddy's assignment, as he should have done.

He left Assioutt in better heart and reached the Great Oasis without setback, but at Beris, at the southern edge of the Oasis, where he was to plunge into the desert again, he decided to leave most of his party behind and press on with just a hundred men.[21] He took the risk of being unable to defend himself against any enemy that he might meet, but he considered that he had too little food and water and too few transport animals to go on with all his men. Information about the rest of the expedition is scanty, and we do not know whether or not he achieved his objectives, but we know that he brought his small force safely to Selimeh, where he arrived on 25th July.[22] It was on that same day that the British Cabinet approved the Gordon Relief Expedition, and much else paled into insignificance.

# CHAPTER FOUR

## EGYPT AND THE SUDAN (2)
## THE GORDON RELIEF EXPEDITION

WOLSELEY WAS GIVEN COMMAND of the relief expedition. It was July 1884. He was now Lord Wolseley and, as Adjutant General, subordinate in the British Army only to the Commander-in-Chief, the Duke of Cambridge; so that the appointment came as a surprise to many, including himself. He had already drawn up provisional plans for such an expedition, and these he began at once urgently to put into effect. In spite of his drive, however, it was September before he arrived in Cairo and October before he could set out from his base at Wadi Halfa, on Egypt's border with the Sudan. His route was to be along the Nile, but his force was divided into a River Column, using boats, and a Desert Column, which would act independently, mounted on camels.

The expedition concentrated at Korti, about two thirds of the way from Wadi Halfa to Khartoum across the desert but considerably less than that along the Nile, the course of which begins there to describe an arc that swings up to the north-east and round to the south-east; and then the two columns separated. The Desert Column was to cut across country, as along the cord of the arc, to meet the River Column at Metemmeh; and, on its way, it was to secure a water supply for the expedition by setting up a base at the oasis of Jakdu; and it is at Jakdu that Eddy is next heard of on 13th January, 1885.[1] Also at Metemmeh, the expedition expected to find steamers sent down by Gordon from Khartoum.

The Desert Column was commanded by General Sir Herbert Stewart, and next in the chain of command came the dashing Colonel Frederick Burnaby, who had appointed himself to the expedition, though without serious objection from Wolseley.[2] Travelling with the Column was Colonel Sir Charles Wilson, head

**Sudan 1884 – 85**
From: *Sir Garnet Wolseley,* by Halik Kochanski

of Wolseley's Intelligence Department, to whose small party Eddy belonged, and Captain Lord Charles Beresford, RN. Wilson's orders were to move on with his party to Khartoum ahead of the rest of the expedition, in one of Gordon's steamers, with Beresford; he was to return to Metemmeh with whatever intelligence he had gathered, but his party was to remain with Gordon at Khartoum, to await the arrival of the Relief Expedition.[3]

On 16th January, the Desert Column was approaching the oasis of Abu Klea, not far from Metemmeh, when it found itself facing a large enemy force: the figures vary from source to source, but the men of the Column were heavily outnumbered by the so-called dervishes. A bloody battle was fought the next day, remembered as one in which a British square was broken; though that was not Beresford's memory of it. 'It was a soldier's battle,' Lord Charles wrote, 'because the attack was sudden; it came before the square was formed; and in the stress and tumult orders were useless.'[4] The dervishes finally retired, to repeated cheers from the men of the Column, but casualties were heavy; among the dead was Colonel Burnaby.

Between Abu Klea and Metemmeh there were further, lesser actions, in one of which Sir Herbert Stewart received a fatal wound; and, Burnaby having been killed, the command of the Column devolved upon Sir Charles Wilson. The Column reached the Nile again on 20th January, to find Metemmeh in the hands of the enemy and no sign of the River Column or the steamers. Wilson took up a defensive position at Gubat, a safe distance upriver, and considered his next move: Wolseley had ordered the occupation of Metemmeh, but Wilson doubted the wisdom of putting his much weakened force at further risk for this purpose; and his dilemma was sharpened the following day, by the arrival of four steamers from Khartoum with the news that Gordon was in desperate straits.

Wilson could not hope to save Gordon with his small force, but his appearance at Khartoum with however few men might give the Mahdi pause for thought; and any such pause might see the arrival

**Colonel Sir Herbert Stewart's column crossing the desert**
By an unknown artist
By courtesy of the Director, National Army Museum, London.

of the main body of the Relief Expedition. His departure from Wolseley's plan, providing for the occupation of Metemmeh and the junction of the two Columns, would add to the dangers facing them all, but he must have reminded himself that circumstances alter cases. The decision that he should go to Khartoum having been taken, he spent some time reconnoitring the route upriver and preparing the steamers and their crews. Arrangements had also to be made for the security of the base at Gubat, and the care of the wounded there.

Two steamers finally left Gubat on the morning of 24th January, with Eddy on board one of them. There are several accounts of what followed; fortunately, we have Eddy's own account.[5] When they were close enough to Khartoum, the signaller whom Eddy had with him used a heliograph to contact the garrison, but there was no response. Then the steamers were fired on from forts at Khartoum and Omdurman, and in taking evasive action they became stuck on a sandbank while the firing continued: Eddy claimed that it was thanks to 'the fearfully bad shooting of the enemy' that he survived. The next day, 28th January, when they had come within four hundred yards of Khartoum, they could see that Gordon's flag was no longer flying from Government House.

Hope was not abandoned until after dark that night, when men were put ashore in disguise to obtain proper information, and it was found that Khartoum had indeed fallen to the Mahdi; Gordon had been killed on the morning of 26th January. Eddy left no record of his own feelings at this time, but he referred obliquely to what he had felt in a letter to Gordon's sister two years later.[6] 'I shall never forget our feelings when we arrived near Khartoum and had to turn back:' he wrote, 'and I think you will, perhaps, like to hear that the feeling was fully shared by the black troops on board the steamers.' And he went on to write of the troops' 'spontaneous outbursts of grief'. Like others, Eddy venerated Gordon's memory.[7]

But Wilson's party was still in great danger, and that danger only increased as the steamers headed downriver: there had been the

**The Battle of Abu Klea**
By William Barns Wollen
By courtesy of the Director, National Army Museum, London.

usual seasonal fall in the river level, and the dervishes took every opportunity of attacking from the banks. First one steamer and then the other was wrecked, and on 31$^{st}$ January the party was obliged to make camp and prepare to defend itself on an island two miles long and three quarters of a mile wide. That evening, Eddy set out with twelve men, rowing in an open boat, to raise the alarm at Gubat, forty miles away. There was an enemy fort to be passed, and they drifted passed it with shipped oars at the darkest time of night, but were seen and fired on. No harm was done, however, and they reached Gubat in the early hours of the following morning.

Colvile recorded this episode in the official *History of the Sudan Campaign* without comment:[8] Beresford made more of it in his memoirs.[9] Lord Charles had been forced to stay behind at Gubat by illness, and he was the first to be able to welcome Eddy back. He slept on board the steamer *Safieh*. 'Very early on the morning of 1$^{st}$ February,' he wrote, 'I was awakened by a voice hailing the *Safieh*. I ran to the rail, and there, in the first light of the dawn was a boat, and Stuart Wortley's face was lifted to mine. He climbed aboard. "Gordon is killed and Khartoum has fallen", he said'.[10] Beresford's considered judgement is recorded later in the book: 'Stuart Wortley and his men risked death every mile of the way; and their voyage deserves to be remembered as a bold, determined and gallant achievement.'[11]

Wilson and his party were rescued by Beresford, though not without difficulty, and the Desert Column and the River Column were then extricated from the dangerous positions in which they were both placed: it remained for the British Government to decide what, in the new circumstances, should be done about the Sudan. Wolseley, bitterly disappointed by the failure of the Relief Expedition, wished to fight on and destroy the Mahdi's power, and public opinion in England was behind him. At first, the Cabinet, too, perhaps against its collective better judgement, was inclined to give Wolseley his head; but then it was distracted by the 'Great Game' and the prospect of war with Russia over Afghanistan.

There was a diplomatic interlude for Eddy in the summer and autumn of 1885. Sir Henry Drummond Wolff was sent to Turkey on a Special Mission, to explore the options for the future of Egypt and the Sudan, still supposedly part of the Ottoman Empire, and Eddy was sent with him as Military Attaché. The outcome of the discussions and negotiations, which continued at Constantinople and Cairo until long after he had had anything to do with them, was disappointing;[12] but he left the mission with his reputation enhanced. 'He is full of go and ability and promises to have a very distinguished career,' Wolff told Lord Wharncliffe.[13] It was for his services to this mission that he was appointed CMG.

Then came the last battle of the Sudan campaign, at which Eddy was present. By this time, Wolseley had handed over his command to General Sir Frederick Stephenson, and the Mahdi had died but had been replaced by one of his followers, the Khalifa. The Mahdi had planned to invade Egypt; and, Wolseley's force having moved back to Wadi Halfa, after the debacle of the Relief Expedition, the Khalifa moved forward; but at Ginnis, not far from Wadi Halfa, on 30th December, 1885, an Anglo-Egyptian force under Stephenson routed the dervish horde. The victory was complete, and according to Sir Evelyn Baring, writing later as Lord Cromer, it taught the enemy the most salutary lesson that it had had to learn in the campaign.[14]

By this time, too, Sir Evelyn Wood had been succeeded as Sirdar by General Sir Francis Grenfell, on whose staff Eddy spent the last days of the Sudan Campaign. The end of the campaign was marked by the withdrawal of British troops to the Assouan (Aswan), and in a jaunty letter to Lord Wharncliffe, headed 'On the Nile' '7th April, 1886'[15] Eddy wrote of 'a cheery party' headed by Grenfell, making its way downriver to Assouan ahead of the troops. In this same letter, he referred to his hopes of marrying a young lady called Muriel, identified only as the daughter of 'Lady K'.[16] Miss Vesey had evidently been forgotten.

# CHAPTER FIVE

## MARRIAGE AND THE ARMY

WHILE EDDY and Lord Charles Beresford were serving together with the Gordon Relief Expedition, Louisa, Marchioness of Waterford was having to consider the future of Highcliffe, her home in Hampshire. In August 1885, while Eddy was in Turkey with Sir Henry Drummond Wolff,[1] the Prince of Wales visited Highcliffe; and he took the opportunity of suggesting to Lady Waterford that she should leave the place to Lord Charles, her late husband's nephew. She explained that it was a Stuart place: it had been built by her father, Charles Stuart, Lord Stuart de Rothesay, a grandson of John Stuart, Earl of Bute; and it must go to one of his family.[2] It seems to have been Lord Wharncliffe who suggested Eddy.[3]

Eddy was back in England in the summer of 1886, with the substantive rank of captain and the brevet rank of major;[4] and 'a tour of Regimental duty in the 2$^{nd}$ Battalion' followed.[5] This duty did not interfere unduly with his social life, and by the end of the year he was talking of marriage again, this time to Eva, daughter of Lord and Lady Aveland.[6] Lord Wharncliffe and Lady Waterford both seem to have approved of Eva; their correspondence shows that by the end of 1887 they had at least pencilled the couple in at Highcliffe.[7] It was not for another two years, however, that Eddy was told that he was Lady Waterford's heir, and by that time his marriage plans had changed once more. Sometime at the end of 1887 or the beginning of 1888 Lord Aveland put a stop to his relationship with Eva.[8]

A crisis in Eddy's father's affairs, provoked by his drinking, occurred in the summer of 1888, to add to Eddy's unhappiness, and he wrote to Lord Wharncliffe on 24$^{th}$ July for advice.[9] He saw the situation as hopeless, not discouraged in that view by what he had heard from one of the doctors, and he thought the time had come for

**Louisa, Marchioness of Waterford**
Photograph by courtesy of Ian Stevenson.

his mother to be relieved of the burden of his father's care. There were letters to Lord Wharncliffe from other members of the family; in the same vein; his sister, Cicely, Lady Montagu of Beaulieu, urged him, as head of the family, to take whatever legal and practical steps could be taken.[10] The doctors' opinion was that treatment could not be made compulsory,[11] but Francis was persuaded to hand over the management of his affairs to others.[12]

There is a sad letter in the records from Eddy to one of his friends, dated only 18th May but thought to belong to 1889, in which he wrote of having 'no home, no money and no object in life'.[13] Fortunately, all that was to change: he was then at the Staff College at Camberley, through which he was to pass successfully to staff appointments; and it was in that same year that he heard he was to inherit Highcliffe.[14] There is no mention of Violet Guthrie in the letters from Eddy to Lord Wharncliffe that have survived, but we know that they first met as early as 1885;[15] they were married on 5th February, 1891, at St Peter's Church, Eaton Square, in the presence of both of his parents, the Wharncliffes and other members of the family.[16] Lady Waterford was not there: her health was failing rapidly, and she died on 12th May, 1891.[17]

Violet left accounts of her own family in her books.[18] She was the daughter of James Guthrie, a Scot from what was then Forfarshire and is now Angus, who made his mark in the City of London. Her mother was Elinor Stirling, a great beauty, the daughter of Admiral Sir James Stirling, first Governor of Western Australia. She was the seventh of nine children, brought up partly in Portland Place and partly in the country, near Guildford, in Surrey. Her father died young and her mother later married Forster Arbuthnot, a retired Indian civil servant, who seems to have been a success as a stepfather. It was a close family, and Violet wrote fondly of her brothers and sisters, perhaps particularly fondly of her sister Lilias, who married Rennell Rodd, diplomat and scholar.

She also left accounts of the social circle into which she moved with Eddy. At the centre was Edward, Earl of Wharncliffe, a wealthy

**Highcliffe Castle**
Copyright: Simmons Aerofilms Limited.

man with estates in Yorkshire, Cornwall and Scotland, and interests in coal-mining and the railways: he 'possessed sound judgement and a liberal mind', but had 'little of the idealist about him'.[19] Susan, Countess of Wharncliffe, was 'witty and wise, and Junoesque in her beauty...'[20] They were generous hosts: their shooting parties at Wortley were famous, but it is not surprising to find that Violet preferred their dinner parties in London. 'At Wharncliffe House in Curzon Street a dinner was, as a matter of course, a model of culinary art, besides, an occasion for conversational brilliance – from eight until midnight and later.'[21]

Another visitor to Wortley who had something to say about it in her memoirs was Susan Buchan, Lady Tweedsmuir. 'Aunt Susan and Uncle Edward were people whose mode of life could only have existed in the late Victorian era,' she wrote. 'They moved with majesty and had rigid and exacting standards of behaviour and conduct.'[22] She was impressed by the pictures, as were other visitors. Lord Wharncliffe was a patron of the arts, and the records contain letters to him from Frederick Leighton, John Everett Millais and Effie Millais, Edward Poynter and Edward Burne-Jones,[23] whose great work *King Cophetua and the Beggar Maid*, now at Tate Britain, went to Wortley from the Grosvenor Gallery Exhibition of 1884.[24] The same batch of letters contains several from Lillie Langtry.

Highcliffe was different. It had been built during the short reign of William IV, 1830-1837, and it had changed little, externally or internally, since then: it still reflected in every detail of its flamboyant architecture and its furnishings the personality and style of life of Lord Stuart de Rothesay. There were portraits of his forebears and the great men of nineteenth century Europe, many of whom he had known; there was exquisite French furniture; and, most telling, there was a huge library of books and manuscripts, with the records of the thirty years of his diplomatic career. 'But', said Violet, 'there were of course no bathrooms (those came much later), no hot water except from the basement, no electric light, no central heating!'[25]

**Edward Montagu-Stuart-Wortley-Mackenzie
3rd Baron and 1st Earl of Wharncliffe**
By Frank Sargent
By courtesy of the National Portrait Gallery, London.

Violet added to her catalogue of deficiencies the note that 'ESW had a passion for entertaining!'[26] And not long after they had taken possession of Highcliffe, they organised a house party for the Duke and Duchess of Connaught. The Duke was Queen Victoria's son, GOC Southern Command and Colonel-in-Chief of the King's Royal Rifles, and so entitled to some consideration, while the Duchess was known to be shy; but all went well, as far as Violet was aware. 'It all went swimmingly,' she said, ' – at least I hope everyone got hot water for their baths of a morning; though I pitied the poor housemaids who had to carry every drop in cans to the bedrooms situated atop various staircases.'[27]

Eddy's career prevented him from making the most of Highcliffe for some time: his first staff appointment after his course at the Staff College was as Brigade Major in Malta; but between whiles there were brief spells of duty elsewhere. He and Violet spent the years 1893-1896 in Malta, where their home was one of the grand houses that had belonged to the Knights of the Order of St John and their friends were largely members of the British service community. There were visits to other islands and countries in the Mediterranean, and on one occasion Eddy obtained leave to race a pony at a sporting event in Egypt. 'My husband's General must have been very tolerant,' Violet observed.[28]

This occasion remained in Violet's memory for another reason. Violet's brother-in-law, Rennell Rodd, was on the staff of the British Agent and Consul-General, Lord Cromer, the former Sir Evelyn Baring, and both he and Violet's sister, Lilias, liked him. When the Stuart Wortleys were invited to dinner with the Rodds by Lady Cromer, therefore, they expected to enjoy the evening, but from the first Lord Cromer gave them the impression that he was bored. Conversation flagged at dinner and failed soon afterward. Their host stood in front of the mantelpiece, with his eyes on the clock, Violet recalled. 'As it struck ten, he said "Good night" firmly. The guest withdrew hurriedly as though a pistol had been presented at their heads.'[29]

Soon after their return to England, Eddy was appointed to the staff of the then Sirdar, Kitchener, now General Sir Herbert Kitchener, and found himself in Egypt again. This time, Violet was left behind; she now had three children to care for, Rothesay, born in 1892, Louise born in 1893, and Elizabeth, always known as Bettine, born in 1896.

# CHAPTER SIX

## EGYPT AND THE SUDAN (3)

## OMDURMAN

EDDY WON THE DSO at Omdurman in 1898; it was the highest honour that he was to be awarded. In a sense, therefore, the campaign that led up to the battle, more particularly its last days, marked the highest point of his career.

The Sudan had been abandoned to the Mahdists, by then led by the Khalifa, in 1885; ten years later the British Government found itself having to decide whether or not to mount a campaign to recover it: shame for what had amounted to defeat at the hands of the dervishes and failure to save General Gordon were motivating factors, but more compelling was the growth of French influence in the region. The decision to act was taken in 1896, and it was taken in response to an upsurge of imperialist sentiment in England and a call for military assistance from Italy. The Italian colony of Eritrea was having to fight off attacks from Abyssinia, and there was reason to fear intervention on behalf of the Abyssinians by the Mahdists.

The campaign was intended to be an all-Egyptian affair, and at first there was no problem about that; the Egyptian Army had been re-organised and re-equipped and the Egyptian treasury refilled in recent years. General Sir Herbert Kitchener, who had succeeded Sir Francis Grenfell as Sirdar, had the command, and he was responsible to Lord Cromer, as Agent and Consul-General. Kitchener's Director of Intelligence was Eddy's old friend and colleague Reginald Wingate, of whom it was said when the campaign was over, 'Whatever there was to know, Colonel Wingate surely knew it.'[1] Wingate eventually succeeded Kitchener as Sirdar, and was later Governor-General of the Sudan.

**Major Edward Stuart Wortley KRRC**
Photograph by courtesy of
The Royal Green Jackets Museum, Winchester

During 1896 the northernmost province of the Sudan, Dongola, was retaken, with its capital, the town of Dongola, but there was no further action for some time. The British Government was ultimately in charge, and some in the Cabinet took the view that there was no need to do more. Then reports from Wingate's agents raised the spectre of a hostile alliance of the Mahdists, the Abyssinians and the French,[2] and agreement was soon achieved: the goal should be Khartoum. But time had not been altogether wasted, since transport would be a major problem of the campaign and work had begun on a railway from Wadi Halfa to the south; a Gunboat Flotilla was already in existence, though it was to be enlarged and given new and better-designed vessels.

The commander of the Gunboat Flotilla was Commander Colin Keppel, RN, and according to *Who Was Who* his second-in-command was Eddy.[3] The *Army List* tells us that Eddy was 'Staff Officer to the Gunboat Flotilla'.[4] Eddy himself said he commanded a gunboat.[5] We have few details of his activities with the flotilla, but one story that he told was recorded by Violet.[6] On board a captured enemy vessel, Eddy discovered a box that had belonged to General Gordon; it had Gordon's name on it, and Eddy remembered it as one that he himself had packed for the General. 'But instead of a major-general's uniform', Violet quoted Eddy as saying, 'there was the helmet and coat of mail and dervish emir.' The box went to Gordon's sister and its contents to Highcliffe.

Khartoum was chosen as the goal early in 1897. In August the Sirdar's forces re-took Abu Hamed, and in September the Friendlies, a force of friendly Arabs, seized Berber, second in strategic importance only to Omdurman; the importance of Khartoum had been largely symbolic since its destruction in 1885. From Berber on 15th September, 1897, Eddy wrote to Wingate with a request for new boots, adding to this a certain amount of information that may have been of more interest to the Director of Intelligence.[7] Gunboats had sailed to within twenty-eight miles of Metemmeh and shelled a Mahdist post at a place called Kitiab, and the Nile was clear of the enemy as far as Shendi, a town opposite

**Gunboat 'Melik'**

One of a flotilla of gunboats that took part in the campaign leading up to the Battle of Omdurman.
Copyright: the National Maritime Museum.

Metemmeh. 'I wish gunboats could go up the Atbara', Eddy remarked, at the end of his letter. 'I am afraid we have now entered upon a period of "masterly inactivity".'

The crux of the campaign had been reached, as Kitchener put it later.[8] Wingate had had no difficulty in discovering that the Khalifa was hell-bent on a return to Berber, while the Egyptian army was already south of the town; and the Sirdar called for British reinforcements: the affair was no longer to be all-Egyptian. A Mahdist force set out for Berber from Omdurman, striking east into the desert before moving north in order, at one and the same time, to avoid Fort Atbara, Kitchener's great base at the confluence of the rivers Nile and Atbara, and to outflank the Sirdar's army, but it came to a halt in a strong defensive position on the course of the river Atbara; it was short of supplies, particularly water. Gunboats could not reach it because the river had dried up, and such was the strength of its position that Kitchener hesitated to attack it.

Kitchener could not advance with this threat on his flank. His own advisers could not agree on what should be done, and neither could his political masters in Cairo and London; and he finally decided that he must attack, come what might. The Battle of Atbara was fought on 8th April, 1898, and it resulted in a complete victory for the British and the Egyptians. The Khalifa's army at Omdurman showed no sign of issuing forth, and Kitchener's Anglo-Egyptian army was able to rest during the hottest time of the year in 'the vast tented city that had sprung up south of Berber'.[9] The way was clear to Khartoum, and Kitchener had been given time to make thorough plans for the last phase of the campaign.

In August 1898 Kitchener concentrated his army at Wad Hamed, sixty miles from Khartoum; and from Wad Hamed on 26th August Eddy set out on an assignment that Winston Churchill, who was there, described as 'one of considerable peril'.[10] The Anglo-Egyptian army was to approach Omdurman along the west bank of the Nile, while Eddy was to lead a force of Friendlies in parallel with it along the east bank, to protect its flank. Eddy's command

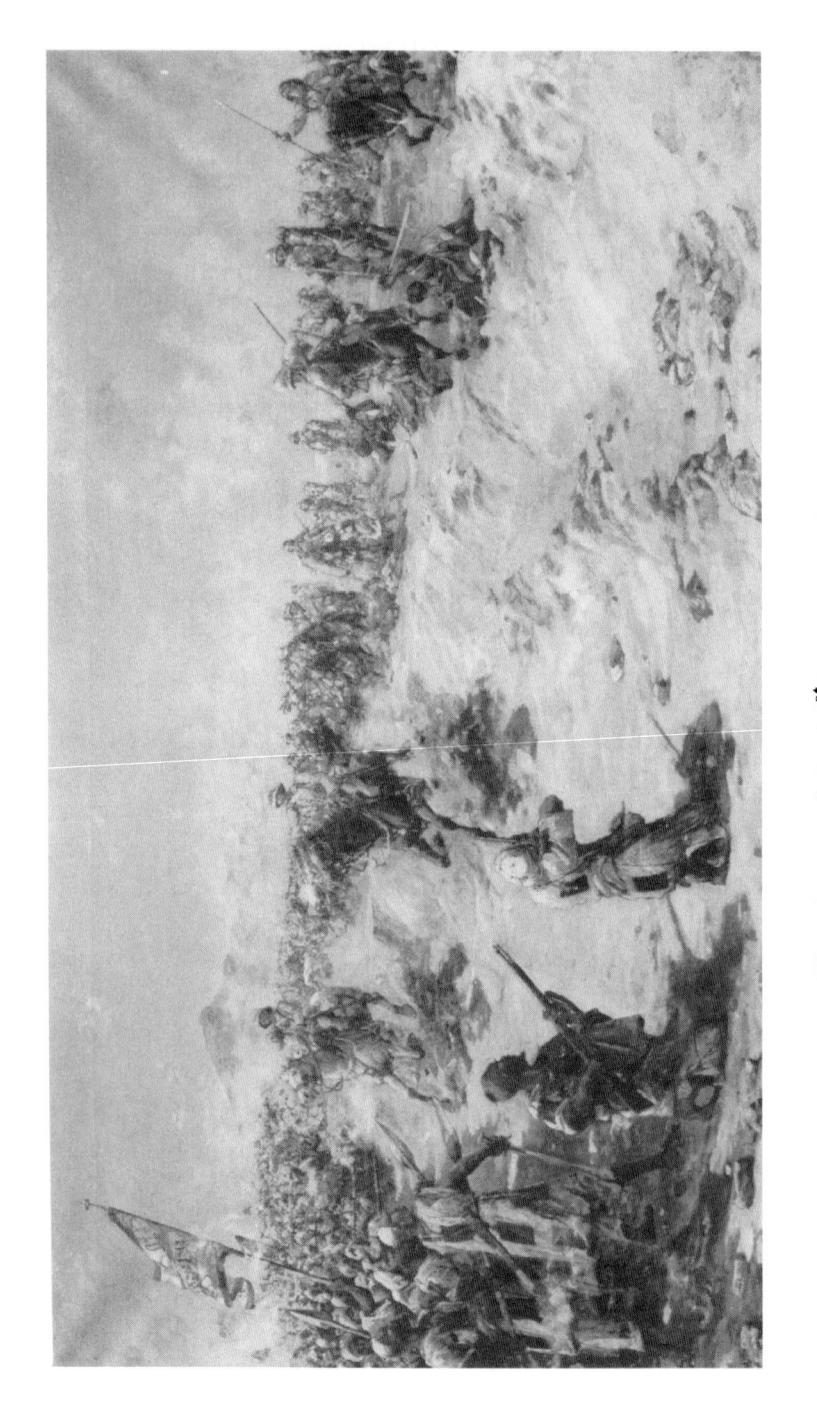

**The charge of the 21st Lancers at Omdurman**
By E.M.Hale
By courtesy of the Director, National Army Museum, London.

consisted of between two and three thousand Arab irregulars, from different tribes and traditions, not all of them disciplined or trustworthy, and he had with him one other British officer, Lieutenant Wood.[11] Eddy had the advantage that he spoke Arabic and had led irregulars before.

He and his men had what was called 'a brush with some dervishes' on 30th August,[12] but it was not until the next day, 1st September, the day before the great battle, that they were involved in a significant action. This action was described briefly by Kitchener in a despatch that was published in *The London Gazette*.[13] The east bank of the Nile opposite Omdurman had to be cleared of the enemy, and howitzers had then to be landed from gunboats and positioned to fire across the river into the city. 'After two forts had been destroyed and the villages gallantly cleared by the irregulars,' the Sirdar reported, 'the howitzers were landed in a good position on the right bank from which an effective fire was opened on Omdurman...'

Churchill had more than this to say about it.[14] The forts and villages were shelled by the gunboats; then Eddy sent his men in to the attack. He sent his least reliable men in first, and his judgement of their fighting qualities was justified as they gingerly approached the nearest buildings. 'Arrived within 500 yards', said Churchill, 'they halted, and began to discharge their rifles into the air; they also indulged in frantic dances expressive of their fury and valour, but declined to advance further.' Then Eddy sent in men of the Jaalin tribe, who moved forward slowly and methodically, surrounding forts and houses one by one, and slaughtering every man they found in them. The howitzer battery was brought ashore to begin its bombardment without incident.

The Battle of Omdurman was fought on 2nd September: the Khalifa was defeated and Mahdism was destroyed. The outcome can never have been seriously in doubt, since the Anglo-Egyptian army's weapons were greatly superior to those of the Mahdist hordes, and the Sirdar was a better tactician than the Khalifa, but the Mahdists fought with great courage. 'It was the last day of Mahdism, and the greatest', said the *Daily Mail's* correspondent, George Steevens.[15]

When the battle was seen to be lost, however, the Mahdists fled, and the Khalifa was obliged to follow in order to avoid capture; he left the city of Omdurman as Kitchener entered it.

The Friendlies' task during the battle was to co-operate with the Gunboat Flotilla in the protection of the army's flanks and rear; there was little enemy activity on the east bank, but towards the end of the day Eddy found the Friendlies facing men from the Khalifa's tribe, the Baggara, and he was pleased to have Jaalins with him. 'Luckily for him,' Steevens noted, 'the opposition was not severe, for most of the Friendlies bolted at the sight of a Baggara, as everybody knew they would. The Jaalin, however, behaved well.'[16]

Before the Friendlies were disbanded the sheikh of the Jaalin presented Eddy with an amulet, in the form of a turquoise pendant inscribed with words from the Koran, which he said had been passed down from generation to generation in his family. This grizzled warrior had been scornful of the young British officer at first, but had become devoted to him.[17] The pendant now belongs to the Royal Green Jackets Museum at Winchester.

It is to the period of Eddy's return to England after Omdurman that the cartoon and profile of him in *Vanity Fair* belong. The suggestion in the profile that he used the militia as a backdoor into the regular army has already been discussed, and all that needs to be said about that here is that it does not inspire confidence in the accuracy of the reporting. However, *Vanity Fair* featured him in a series called 'Men of the Day', and it can be reasonably inferred that he was a well-known figure, at least in certain social circles. His career, so far, was reviewed; what came next in the profile is interesting because it is new.

> Withal he is a very modest hero, who is far more ready to fight the foes of England than he is to talk in

a drawing room. He is also a handsome fellow who is good at polo, keen on shooting and fond of fishing. He likes sailing so well that he once lived on a yacht for five months at a stretch.[18]

# CHAPTER SEVEN

# THE BOER WAR (1)

THE BOER WAR began in October 1899. Its immediate cause was the denial of basic rights to immigrants and foreign workers, the Uitlanders, by the Boers of the Transvaal; but that problem might have been dealt with peacefully if the more basic question of power in South Africa had not been to the fore in men's minds. There had been reason to hope that the British and the Dutch could live amicably together, an end for which Cecil Rhodes had worked; but Rhodes himself had virtually destroyed all such hope in 1885, when he attempted to organise an uprising of the Uitlanders, with help from his British South Africa Company. The plan was aborted, but not in time to stop the so-called Jameson Raid, which united Dutch opinion against the British.

Eddy volunteered for service in South Africa straightaway,[1] and he was appointed to the staff of the Commander-in-Chief of the British Army in South Africa, General Sir Redvers Buller, VC, as Assistant Adjutant-General.[2] But he was ordered to proceed to Cape Town via Naples, and there to take on board several hundred mules, with their Italian handlers. During the voyage the muleteers treated their animals so badly that many of them died, and nothing Eddy said or did made any difference to their behaviour until he had them flogged. Corporal punishment had been abolished in the British Army, and at Cape Town Eddy was warned to expect a court martial; but, according to Violet, he got away with the plea that the muleteers were not soldiers of the Queen.[3]

The Boers had invaded the British colony of Natal before Buller had arrived in South Africa, and the Natal Field Force, under General Sir George White, had come to grief: half had had to surrender, and the other half had been cooped up under siege at Ladysmith. In Cape Colony, also British, at the same time,

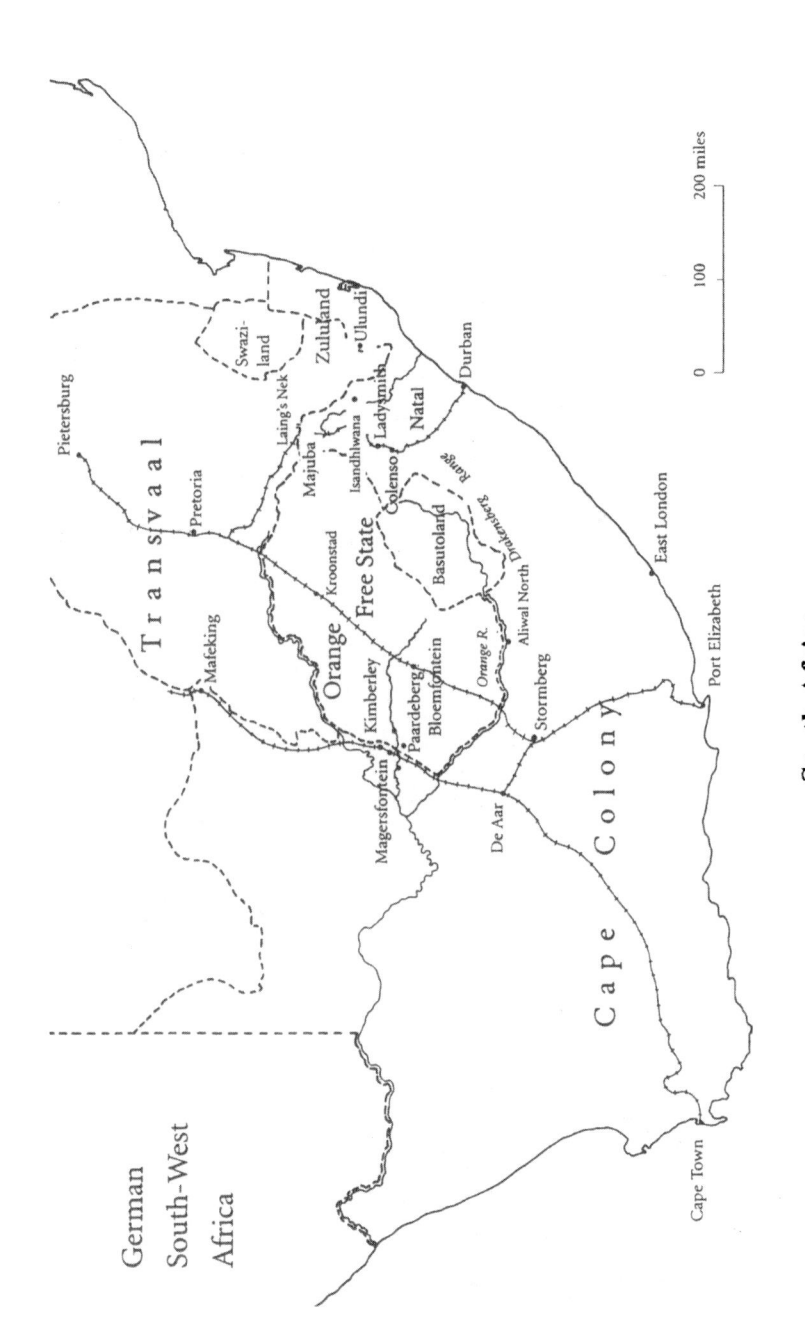

**South Africa**
From: *Sir Garnet Wolseley*, by Halik Kochanski

Kimberley and Mafeking had been placed under siege. Buller had intended to strike at the Boer republics of the Orange Free State and the Transvaal with his entire Army Corps; faced with the situation as it was, however, he split the Corps and sent Sir General William Gatacre to raise the siege of Mafeking, General Lord Methuen to relieve Kimberley and General Sir Francis Clery to save Ladysmith. Buller himself followed Clery to Natal.

The war for Eddy thus began in Natal, where Buller, having taken personal command in the colony, struggled for nearly three months to reach Ladysmith. Between the British force and its objective, to the north, lay a formidable natural obstacle, fortified and held by the Boer commander Louis Botha: there was, first, the Tugela river, on which stood the village of Colenso; secondly, beyond the river, there was a multi-tiered range of hills. A large military base had been set up at Frere, a hamlet on the railway line from Durban to Ladysmith, twelve miles south of Colenso. A forward base had been set up at Chieveley, halfway between Frere and Colenso.

One of Eddy's first tasks was to raise a Volunteer Corps of Stretcher Bearers, and the inference is that he was in charge of this corps during the Battle of Colenso: the official record of his service tells us that he both raised and commanded it;[4] and in a letter to a friend after the battle he said it was still his.[5] One of the best accounts of this corps was written by the surgeon Frederick Treves, later Sir Frederick Treves, who was there. According to Treves, it consisted of two thousand men, though Eddy put the figure at twelve hundred, and it was made up of 'all sorts and conditions of men – labourers, mechanics, 'gentlemen', dock loafers, seamen, dentists, a chemist or two, a lawyer or two, tram drivers, clerks, miners, and shop assistants'.[6]

It was not a promising body of men: first and foremost, they had little in common, particularly not motivation. Many who had lost their jobs as a result of the war, including refugees from the Transvaal, wanted work; others were looking for excitement. No doubt there were some who were motivated by altruism or even

**General Sir Redvers Buller VC**
Photograph by courtesy of the Image Library, Public Record Office, Kew.

patriotism, and the existence of the corps certainly served the purpose of British propaganda: here were men of various racial groups, unwilling or unable to fight for whatever reasons, who had nevertheless chosen to work actively for a British victory in a colonial war. Among them was a group from the Indian community in Natal; this was led by a young lawyer, who was to become known to the world as Mahatma Ghandi.[7]

Treves described the men as 'wild and shabby looking, disordered, unsymmetrical, and bizarre'.[8] Their behaviour would have marked them out, at first, if their appearance had not: most were lost in the company of their new comrades and the setting of an army camp; many were either unable to adapt themselves to the changes in their lives or were unacceptable to their colleagues in some other way, and these had to be sent away. They were the butt of the soldiers' humour until they had been transformed into an efficient working unit, as eventually they were, thanks to Eddy and the Principal Medical Officer, Colonel Thomas Gallwey, who greatly impressed Eddy.[9] 'They were the means of saving many lives and an infinite amount of pain,' Treves wrote of them in the end.[10]

Ambulances were used, but they could not cope easily with the rough terrain. Treves wrote of these vehicles, hooded wagons, each drawn by ten mules, 'rocking and groaning over the uneven veldt, like staggering men...'[11] There were six bearers to each stretcher, and their duty was to carry the wounded to the nearest dressing-station or field hospital and on, if necessary, to the main hospital or the railway. It was an arduous and dangerous duty: the bearers had sometimes to carry their patients twenty-five miles; and many of them, too, were killed or wounded. It was also a gruesome duty. Treves, writing after the Battle of Colenso, said he did not think any surgeon, accustomed to gruesome sights, would want to remember what he had seen that day.[12]

The Battle of Colenso, on 15th December, 1899, was a disaster, largely because Buller based his orders on false assumptions. 'Two days bombardment elicited no reply from the Boers: and it was

**Watching the Battle of Colenso**

Photograph by courtesy of the Director, National Army Museum, London.

therefore assumed that they were not present in strength,' Eddy wrote to a friend on 26$^{th}$ December. 'The whole force was then ordered to make a frontal attack against the strongest position it is possible to conceive...The result has been a terrible loss of life: and a reverse which has lowered our prestige very considerably.'[13] And, to make matters worse, it came within the same 'Black Week' as two other disasters: both Gatacre and Methuen had been defeated. One of the heroes of Colenso was Lieutenant Frederick Roberts, who was killed and awarded a posthumous VC; he was the son of Field Marshal Lord Roberts, VC, of whom more was now to be heard.

Christmas 1899 was not a wholly cheerful occasion for the British force in Natal, but it was marked as appropriately as possible. Winston Churchill, in South Africa as correspondent of *The Morning Post*, had arrived at Frere on Christmas Eve, after his dramatic escape from a Boer prison in Pretoria, and he described the scene in one of his books. The British and the Boers left each other in peace for the day, and religious services were held by both sides; an ironical state of affairs to which Churchill drew attention without comment.[14] On the British side there were then 'athletic sports, an impromptu military tournament, and a gymkhana', followed by Christmas dinner.[15] Eddy and Churchill had breakfast together on Boxing Day, and Eddy was much impressed by the story that Churchill had to tell.[16]

Buller was badly shaken by Colenso, and in his shaken state he exposed himself to a further blow. In messages to the Secretary for War, the Marquess of Lansdowne, in London, and to Sir George White, at Ladysmith, he made what was interpreted as the proposal that Ladysmith should be abandoned, and the Cabinet promptly replaced him as Commander-in-Chief in South Africa by Lord Roberts, leaving him the command in Natal. It has been cogently argued that he was, in fact, proposing a change of strategy that would have put pressure on the Boers elsewhere and drawn the besieging force away from Ladysmith,[17] but if this is the case he certainly expressed himself in a way that caused misunderstanding.

**Winston Churchill in 1899**
Photograph by courtesy of the Image Library, Public Record Office, Kew.

On 6th January, 1900, the Boers made an attempt to storm Ladysmith, and it was clear to Buller that time was running out for the besieged town. Having recovered himself, he planned what was to be a westward outflanking movement against the Boers' position at Potgieters. General Sir Charles Warren, recently arrived from England with reinforcements, was to lead the main force, which would cross the river at Trickhardt's Drift, and break through the hills behind it, west of their highest point, Spion Kop, to the plain beyond. When this force was in position, on the Boers' flank, Buller would launch a frontal attack, crossing the river at Potgieter's Drift. Warren and his men set out on 10th January, and Eddy, who had rejoined his regiment, was with them.[18]

The operation did not go according to plan, and Warren decided to seize Spion Kop, from which he hoped to be able to dominate the surrounding country; he would control the route through the hills and perhaps, if heavy guns could be dragged up the hill, drive the Boers back to the plain. The hill was taken and defensive positions were prepared during the night of 23rd January, but next morning, when a mist had cleared, it became obvious that the preparations that had been made were quite inadequate. The Boers counter-attacked and a particularly bloody battle was fought; it was 'the old style "soldiers' battle" of pulped faces, of headless trunks, of men fighting like animals'.[19] Fighting went on all day, but the position was untenable, and when darkness fell again the survivors withdrew.

The British were defeated at the Battle of Spion Kop, and Buller was frustrated in his second attempt to reach Ladysmith. Eddy was not one of the detachment of Warren's force that fought for the hill; but there was action elsewhere at the same time, and one of Violet's stories probably refers to this. According to Violet, a shell burst in Eddy's tent when he was lying on his bed, but he was unscathed; again according to Violet, he attributed his escape to the protection of a talisman that he was wearing.[20] This was the pendant that had been given to him by the sheikh of the Jaalin after Omdurman.

**General Sir Frederick Roberts VC**
Later Field Marshal The Earl Roberts VC
Photograph by courtesy of the Image Library, Public Record Office, Kew.

Another of Violet's stories has it that a hen, known to Eddy as Emily, 'came regularly each morning to his tent in the neighbourhood of Spion Kop, and laid an egg for his breakfast'.[21]

On 5th February, Buller tried again, this time with an attack on Vaal Krantz, a ridge of hills about five miles east of Spion Kop, but again he was forced to retire. We know that Eddy was at Vaal Krantz,[22] but we do not know what part he played in the operation. By this time, Buller's men, Eddy among them, were losing confidence in him; and Eddy's views had not changed when he wrote to his father's cousin, Margaret Talbot, on 1st April, after the relief of Ladysmith. ' I am afraid no one has any confidence in Buller:' he wrote, 'and when the war is over, his conduct of the operations in Natal will appear in a worse light than is at present shown.'[23] The credit for the relief of Ladysmith, Eddy told Margaret Talbot, belonged to her brother-in-law, General Neville Lyttelton.[24]

Ladysmith was finally relieved on 28th February, after a series of further actions, begun on 12th February. East of Colenso the course of the river took it in a northerly or north-easterly direction through a gorge, cutting off the Boers' left flank, which lay on the south or south-east bank. There were hills on this side of the river too: Hlangwane, closest to the river, and then a group, including the highest of them all, Monte Cristo. In the first part of the operation, Buller's plan was to take these hills, one by one, in an eastward outflanking movement, which would have the particular advantage of giving him a dominating position above the Boers' flank. This was completed on 19th February, with the capture of Hlangwane.

Eddy was given command of the Rifle Reserve Battalion, which Buller explained in his despatches was 'a scratch regiment made up by combining the drafts for the three rifle battalions in Ladysmith';[25] it was also known as the Composite Rifles.[26] He told Margaret Talbot that he was fighting with the battalion for twelve days,[27] which means that he was involved in most of the action. The first mention of his name in the records places him at Colenso on 20th February, when he led his men into the village unopposed:[28]

**Our Soldiers firing volleys to keep the Boers down in their trenches on the Tugela Heights**
Photograph by courtesy of the Image Library, Public Record Office, Kew

nothing else was as easy, but Buller was impressed by what he achieved. ' I was much struck,' he stated in one of despatches, 'by the way in which a battalion made up of the drafts of three regiments, and officered chiefly by Second Lieutenants, worked under his command.'[29]

For the second part of the operation, Buller chose to cross the Tugela near Colenso and then to fight his way north, along a corridor that followed the course of the river before it swung round to the east again. On his left, however was a series of hills, from all of which the Boers fired down on him, the last of them, about five miles from Colenso, was Pieters Hill, where Botha had his main position, and beyond that was Ladysmith. As long as the British had to run the gauntlet of the Boers, the outcome of the whole operation hung in the balance. Then, while the Boers at the southern end of the corridor were kept engaged, part of Buller's force returned across the river and crossed it again opposite the northern end of the corridor, where it took Botha's position at Pieters Hill on 27th February.

The Composite Rifles, meanwhile, were involved in a one of the best-recorded actions of the second part of the operation, if only peripherally. On 23rd February, General Fitzroy Hart, commander of the Irish Brigade, who had a reputation for reckless courage, if not sheer recklessness, attempted to storm the hill that was named after him, Hart's Hill, halfway along the corridor. He began the attempt late in the day and before his full force had assembled; the Boers were well entrenched and were able to fire down on the Irish, who had little cover as they scrambled up the hill. Hart insisted that his men should try and try again, and they were mown down in their hundreds. When night fell, however, Hart still had a hold on the lower slopes.

'That night', Buller recorded, 'the enemy made a heavy attack on our left. There was hard fighting, a good deal of it hand to hand, prisoners being taken and retaken, and several bayonet charges being delivered.'[30] The Rifle Reserve Battalion, under the command of Major Stuart-Wortley, 'behaved very well', he added. Churchill reported the incident in the same terms. 'Sixteen men of Stuart-Wortley's composite battalion of Reservists of the Rifle Brigade and the King's Royal Rifles showed blood on their bayonets in the morning', he remarked.[31] And now, in long retrospect, Eddy's reference to it in the letter to Margaret Talbot that has already been quoted, particularly what he had to say about his work with the bayonet, seems surprisingly uninhibited.[32]

Eddy was present at the action at Pieters Hill on 27th February,[33] but we have no other information about what he did that day. By the end of the day, the way to Ladysmith was open: the hills from which the Boers had wrought havoc had either been seized or evacuated, and the Boers who had not been killed or taken prisoner had disappeared. The next day, watchers at Ladysmith saw the Boers who had surrounded the town moving away to the north; and later in the day Sir George White received a telegram from Buller, announcing his victory and the imminent arrival of the first units of his relieving force. Eddy was present at the relief of Ladysmith, but again we have only that bare information as far as he is concerned.[34] It is reasonable to assume that he took part in Buller's great victory parade three days later.

# CHAPTER EIGHT

## THE BOER WAR (2)

THE TIDE WAS TURNING. Ladysmith and Kimberley had been relieved, Ladysmith on 28$^{th}$ February, 1900, and Kimberley a fortnight earlier, on 15$^{th}$ February. More important than these two successes, however, was the Battle of Paardeberg, in the Orange Free State; at which Lord Roberts arrived in time to snatch victory from the jaws of the defeat that his Chief of Staff, Lord Kitchener, had been facing. The Boer commander, Piet Cronje, surrendered himself and his army to Roberts on 27$^{th}$ February, the day on which Buller broke through the Tugela Heights. A fortnight later, on 13$^{th}$ March, Bloomfontein, the capital of the Orange Free State, was given up without a fight, and in due course, on 28$^{th}$ May, Roberts was to declare the State annexed.

From 2$^{nd}$ March to 20$^{th}$ June, Eddy had the command of the 2$^{nd}$ Battalion of the King's Royal Rifles,[1] about which he wrote to Margaret Talbot, in his letter of 1$^{st}$ April.

> This battalion formed part of the Ladysmith garrison, so we are very weak. The deaths from enteric and dysentery have been quite appalling: and some of the men look like walking ghosts – but the majority are picking up now.[2]

The battalion was part of the 8$^{th}$ Brigade and the 4$^{th}$ Division of the Army of South Africa, and the 4$^{th}$ Division was commanded by General Neville Lyttelton,[3] one of the most competent of the generals in South Africa.

Neville Lyttelton had married Katherine Stuart Wortley; she and Margaret Talbot were sisters, the daughters of James Stuart Wortley, a younger son of 1$^{st}$ Lord Wharncliffe and Solicitor

**General Sir Herbert Kitchener**
Later Field Marshal The Earl Kitchener
Photograph by courtesy of the Image Library, Public Record Office, Kew.

General under Lord Palmerston. Their elder brother was the portraitist Archibald Stuart Wortley, and their younger brother, Charles, was a distinguished public figure, who was raised to the peerage as Lord Stuart of Wortley and married, as his second wife, Sir John Millais's daughter, Alice. Though Lyttelton belonged to the generation ahead of Eddy, he was no more than twelve years older than him. 'It was very nice being under him,' Eddy told Margaret Talbot, 'as he is very friendly to me and I go and sit with him and have long talks. He tells me everything privately.'[4]

Roberts' strategy was now to strike at Pretoria, the capital of the Transvaal, and he took part of Buller's force to make the job easier. Buller was ordered to stay on the defensive in Roberts' rear at first, but as soon as the Ladysmith garrison was fit he obtained permission to go on the offensive again with its diminished force, which included Lyttelton's 4th Division. Meanwhile, Botha and his colleague, Piet Joubert, had fortified the Biggarsberg range of hills to the north, and Christiaan Botha, Louis' brother, had secured the main passes through the Drakensberg mountains, which ran along Natal's border with the Orange Free State to the west and into the Transvaal. But Buller was not to be stopped again.

The direction of Buller's planned route of advance was to the north and then to the west, determined to some extent by his sense of the importance of having the railway between Natal and the Transvaal, as an important means of communication and transport, in British hands. Eddy was afraid that he would make a frontal attack on the Biggarsberg, and be thrown back with heavy losses. Perhaps as a result of his talks with Lyttelton, who was not one of Buller's admirers, he thought Roberts was right, and that the Natal army should stay put for the time being: he believed that the Boers in Natal would retreat as soon as Roberts had advanced far enough to threaten their communications with Pretoria.[5]

Between 10th and 15th May Buller outflanked the Boers at the Biggarsberg in what has been described as 'one of the neatest tactical feats of the war',[6] and between 6th and 12th June he repeated the manoeuvre in the Drakensberg. The Boers had expected him to make for one of the main passes, such as Laing's Nek; he sent part of his force to engage them there and the rest of it to a lesser known pass, which it negotiated without great difficulty. Buller was delighted, and the more so for the fact that Roberts had obviously thought he could not do it: some hours after the Boers had abandoned Laing's Nek, he received a telegram from the Commander-in-Chief, warning him that the nut was too hard to crack. There had been some fighting at the Nek, however, and Eddy had been in action there.[7]

While Buller had been out-manoeuvring the Boers at the Biggarsberg and the Drakensberg, important developments had been taking place in the war elsewhere: Mafeking had been relieved on 17th May, and Pretoria had been surrendered on 5th June. At Pretoria, Roberts was at first able to persuade himself that he had won the war, but all too soon he was obliged to look to his laurels: there was still a Boer army to challenge him in the north; Boer guerrillas were active in the south. In the Orange Free State, known since its annexation as the Orange River Colony, the guerrillas were striking at roads and railway lines and cutting the telegraph wires that ran along them. They were attacking military units, too, and inflicting some humiliating defeats.

The records show that Eddy returned to a staff appointment sometime in June,[8] but they do not tell us whose staff it was: Buller had advanced into the Transvaal, but Eddy is said to have been involved in operations in the Orange River Colony. The records do not tell us, either, what the operations in the Orange River Colony were, but it is at least likely that they were anti-guerrilla. There is a gap in our knowledge of Eddy here. It has been suggested that his attitude towards the army changed after the South African War, or that the army changed and he did not.[9] We do know that even then, in the summer of 1900, he was planning to go into Parliament, if he could find a seat.

Buller continued his advance through the Transvaal, succeeding in re-opening the railway as he did so, and on 7th July he met Roberts at Pretoria. The meeting was notable for several reasons: first, because it marked a stage in the progress of the war; secondly, because he had never met Roberts before; and, thirdly, because the two men were suspicious of each other, and their mutual hostility was to break bounds eventually. There were well-known professional differences, and it would be surprising if Roberts was ever able to forget that it was at the bungled Battle of Colenso that his son was killed. For the time being, however, they were able to work together, and when they met next, on 25th August, it was to prepare for what turned out to be the last big set-piece battle of the war.

The Battle of Belfast, east of Pretoria, on 27th August, was 'a crushing victory' for the British Army in Southern Africa,[10] and a great victory for Buller over Botha.

There was more action in the north of the Transvaal in September and October, but on 25th October Roberts declared that republic, too, annexed, and at the end of October Buller returned to England. In December, more reasonably but no less erroneously than in June, Roberts again judged the war as good as over, and he followed Buller home. Buller's failures counted for more than his successes with Roberts and the British Government, and he received little in the way of reward for his services. Roberts, on the other hand, was given an earldom and a grant of £100,000. It was in November that Eddy went home.[11]

Kitchener succeeded Roberts as Commander-in-Chief in South Africa, but it was not until May 1902 that he was able to bring the war to an end. The Boers regained the upper hand temporarily, relying on guerrilla warfare. Then Kitchener criss-crossed the country with wire fences and built blockhouses along the railways and the fences, thus protecting his communications and his means of transport, particularly the transport of troops, and restricting the guerrillas' freedom of movement; at the same time, he moved families suspected of supporting the guerrillas off their land and into concentration camps, a tactic for which history has found it difficult to forgive him. It became a war of attrition, and eventually the Boers sued for peace.

The relationship between Roberts and Buller deteriorated further until, in October 1901, by which time Roberts was Commander-in-Chief of the British Army, it broke down completely, and the consequences spelled the end of Buller's career. One of Roberts' friends wrote a deliberately provocative letter to *The Times*, about Buller's supposed order to White to surrender Ladysmith. Buller had been refused permission to publish the key telegram, but he so far misjudged his position as to quote from it at an official lunch. This was, perhaps, the opportunity for which Roberts had been waiting: Buller was dismissed from the post that he held at the time and never offered another.

# CHAPTER NINE

## HOME FROM THE BOER WAR

A GENERAL ELECTION had taken place in October 1900, before Eddy returned to England; he had been a candidate nonetheless. It became known as the Khaki Election because the Conservative Government of the Marquess of Salisbury, in calling it, hoped to capitalise on the successes of the Army in South Africa, and the fact that Eddy, a Conservative, it need hardly be said, was still serving in that Army made his absence from the hustings a positive advantage in the eyes of some. Violet canvassed for him: 'great stress was laid on the brave fellow fighting for his country while his no less brave wife appealed for votes', she recalled.[1] 'I do not know how many votes I added to the Conservative score,' she added, 'but we did succeed in lowering the previous Radical majority.'[2]

The constituency was Holmfirth, in the West Riding of Yorkshire, attractive to Eddy because his family was well known there. His opponent was Henry Wilson, a member of the National Liberal Party, who represented Holmfirth continuously from 1885 until he accepted the Chiltern Hundreds in 1912. Wilson was a political radical, and it so happened that he objected to aggressiveness, particularly militarism, in foreign policy.[3] In the previous General Election of 1895, he had attracted 59.1 per cent of the votes, in a turnout of 76.2 per cent of the electorate: in the Khaki Election, his share of the votes fell to 54.7 per cent, in a turnout of 73.4 per cent of the electorate.[4] Perhaps Violet was justified in feeling pleased with herself.

Though Lord Salisbury was Prime Minister, Joseph Chamberlain, Colonial Secretary and chief architect of the war, was the Government's champion in the election. The Liberal Party, led by Sir Henry Campbell-Bannerman, was able to put up against Chamberlain the fiery young David Lloyd-George, but it was badly split and could not hope to win. In the event, there were few changes on either side, but the Government's majority was slightly increased; there was one significant addition to the House of Commons, however, that of Winston Churchill, returned as Member for Oldham. Violet said she first met Churchill at about this time, and sensed that she was in the presence of a remarkable man. 'I think there shone about him some hint of future glory, because, early though it was in his career, the impression he made on me remains indelible.'[5]

Thus, what might have been a turning point in Eddy's career was not. But much had changed or was about to change for him and the England to which he returned from South Africa, and the event that more than any other signified change was the death of Queen Victoria, on 22nd January, 1901.

> The shock of her death struck the nation at a dark hour, when it had just discovered the war, presumed to have been won, was still not in sight of an ending. Men felt that a great epoch had closed. The sky of England had been clouding for years before; what with the collapse of the countryside, the new-born social unrest in the towns, the waning of religious faith, and above all the sense of an uncontrollable transition to the unknown – the feeling that the keys of power were blindly but swiftly transferring themselves to new classes, new types of men, new nations. The queen's death focused it all.[6]

What had changed already for Eddy was the family in which he had been brought up. His parents had died several years earlier, his mother in 1891 and his father in 1893; and his uncle, the Earl of Wharncliffe, died in 1899. His brother, Frank, succeeded to the earldom and the estates that went with it, but he and his other brothers and his sister were treated as if their father had succeeded first, as he would have done if he had lived: Eddy was henceforth styled the Honourable Edward Stuart Wortley. Of his younger brothers, Ralph, next to him in the family, was seeking his fortune in America, and Richard was serving with him in the King's Royal Rifles. His sister Mary, now Lady Mary, was married to the baronet Sir George Cayley.

Life at Wortley Hall and Wharncliffe House, too, had changed with the death of the old Earl, and there is a sense of things left unsaid in Violet's comment that in Curzon Street 'a house where everything was fine, artistically, was closed'.[7] A London house that was still open to Eddy and Violet then was Stratford House, in Stratford Place, halfway along Oxford Street. It belonged to Sir John and Lady Constance Leslie for many years, and they gave it to their daughter, Olive, when she married Violet's brother, Murray. Under both regimes, the hospitality dispensed was lavish, and guests were chosen carefully: 'They were all known to each other, had pursuits in common and a similar outlook on life, were unselfseeking, responsive to anything that called into play imagination and the creative impulse'.[8]

Highcliffe had been let while Eddy was in South Africa, but the family was evidently back in residence in March 1901, since the Visitors' Book shows that Susan Grosvenor was staying with them.[9] Susan Grosvenor was the daughter of Katherine Lyttelton's and Margaret Talbot's sister Caroline, who married Norman Grosvenor. The old Earl of Wharncliffe disapproved of Norman Grosvenor at the time of Caroline's engagement to him, in spite of his suitability otherwise, on the grounds that he had been seen wearing a black tie at a ball.[10] Susan herself married John Buchan, later Lord Tweedsmuir, writer and Governor-General of Canada. The Stuart Wortleys' next guests were Sir John and Lady Constance Leslie,[11] who had known Highcliffe in Lady Waterford's day.

Not far from Highcliffe, at Palace House, Beaulieu, lived Eddy's aunt, his father's sister, Cicely, Lady Montagu. She had supported his father in his troubles, and had always taken an interest in him too. One account has it that he was staying at Palace House in 1889 when, on a visit to Lady Waterford, he was given the first hint that

**The Prince of Wales, later King Edward VII, and The Honourable John Scott Montagu, later 2$^{nd}$ Baron Montagu of Beaulieu, in Scott Montagu's 1899 Daimler at Highcliffe Castle in 1900.**

Photograph by courtesy of the Picture Library, National Motor Museum, Beaulieu.

he was to inherit Highcliffe.[12] The link between Highcliffe and Beaulieu was accidentally recorded for posterity in a much published photograph, taken in 1900: it shows the Prince of Wales, shortly to succeed to the throne as King Edward VII, and John Scott Montagu, Lord Montagu's son, Eddy's cousin, in the latter's '12 hp Daimler'; the background is the port-cochère of Highcliffe Castle.[13]

In the same year and the same car, Scott Montagu, pioneer of motoring, was the first MP to drive a motor vehicle into the precincts of the House of Commons. He was stopped by the policeman on duty and had to appeal to the Speaker. History was being made, and Scott Montagu remarked that the significance of what they were witnessing was not lost on those bystanders whose living depended on the horse.

> The drivers of hansoms and four-wheelers who were there on the cabstand gazed wonderingly, for I expect in the back of their minds they knew that their doom was coming.[14]

It ought to be added that he saw motoring as a means of enriching the lives of all, in due course.

Eddy was not long unemployed. In July 1901, he was appointed Military Attaché to the Embassy at Paris, with the substantive rank of lieutenant-colonel. Soon after his appointment, he received a private message from the King, which was relayed by Rennell Rodd: he was 'to devote all his goodwill to maintaining the most cordial relations with the French Army'.[15]

# CHAPTER TEN

## PARIS AND THE ENTENTE CORDIALE

FOR THREE YEARS precisely, from 13<sup>th</sup> July, 1901, to 12<sup>th</sup> July, 1904,[1] Eddy was British Military Attaché at Paris. There was a family connection with the Embassy: the building was purchased by Lady Waterford's father, on behalf of the British Government, at the First Restoration of the Bourbons, in 1814; he occupied it himself as Ambassador, from 1815 to 1824 as Sir Charles Stuart, and from 1828 to 1830 as Lord Stuart de Rothesay.[2] During the Ancien Régime it was the Hôtel de Charost: it then became the home of Napoleon's sister, Princess Pauline Borghese, from whose agents Charles Stuart bought it. The house is still the British Embassy, and among its contents there are still items that belonged to Pauline Borghese. Lady Waterford was born there in 1818.

The Ambassador during Eddy's term of office was Sir Edmund Monson, a distinguished scholar and a Fellow of All Souls. He was 'a tall white-bearded man, shy and unable to express the kindness in his character'.[3] His despatches displayed his scholarship, in that they were beautifully constructed, but they were prolix; it was once said that, reading one of these despatches, 'one had the sensation of coasting pleasantly downhill on a bicycle that had no brake, and save for an accident was not likely to stop'.[4] Lady Monson was 'all of a twitter, timid and gauche';[5] sadly for Sir Edmund and for his staff, she was not often in Paris. 'Month after month,' Violet wrote of the embassy, 'the reception rooms remained shrouded in dust-covers – the shutters closed.'[6]

Fortunately, the staff were more welcoming than the Ambassador and Ambassadress. Fortunately, too, Eddy found the military attachés at the other embassies congenial, except for his German colleague. This officer assumed that spying was part of Eddy's remit, and made his own intelligence gathering activities a source of

**King Edward VII**

Photograph by courtesy of the National Portrait Gallery, London.

amusement to the *corps diplomatique*. 'It seemed he spent large sums and much time interviewing agents, who all offered, at a price, to put him wise to most important information.'[7] There was no doubt, however, that espionage was an occupational hazard for a diplomat in Paris; before the Stuart Wortleys had been in Paris long they realised that their mail was being interfered with, probably by Violet's maid.

Attendance at the Bastille Day celebrations of 14th July, 1901 must have been one of Eddy's first duties. His military attaché's uniform was not ready, and he appeared at the parade in what Violet called 'his regimental outfit, a Rifleman's black tunic with Atrakhan trimming.'[8] The story may have been embroidered, but the version that was published in Violet's reminiscences has it that the crowd, unfamiliar with his uniform, took him for a Boer and cheered him wildly, with cries of 'Vive les Boers!' At this, his horse took fright and reared, and he, 'as near as possible, fell off under the President's box.'[9]

Violet mentioned specifically only one other of the duties that fell to Eddy, a sad one: that of identifying the body of General Sir Hector MacDonald, who shot himself in a Paris hotel in 1902. MacDonald had risen from the ranks and had distinguished himself in most of the conflicts of his generation, which was Eddy's generation too; but, while serving in Ceylon, he had disgraced himself, in the eyes of his contemporaries, by carrying on a homosexual relationship with a Ceylonese boy. Eddy had been a friend, and he made sure that what was left to be done was done properly. 'With all reverence they laid him to rest,' Violet recorded, 'the French authorities doing their utmost to honour a man who had fought for his country.'[10]

Most of Violet's reminiscences of Paris concern her social life, about which she wrote lovingly and lingeringly. It was difficult for the Stuart Wortleys to establish themselves socially outside the *corps diplomatique*, partly because the rules governing French social life in Paris were arcane, but partly, too, because they had

**The Marquis de Soveral**

Photograph by courtesy of the National Portrait Gallery, London.

arrived at a time when the British were highly unpopular with the French. The new King of England, Edward VII, was about to change all that, but meanwhile they made their own way, and before long they might have claimed that they had arrived in another sense. Indeed, we have the word of the Ambassador that Eddy came through, in the end, with flying colours; and it can be inferred from the context that the same applied to Violet.

Sir Edmund was reporting to the Foreign Secretary, the Marquess of Lansdowne, at the end of Eddy's tenure of office, on 12$^{th}$ July, 1904. 'It is my agreeable duty', he wrote, 'to testify to the universal popularity of Colonel Stuart Wortley, whose social position in Paris has been exceptionally brilliant, and whose hospitality and personal qualities have won him most deservedly general recognition both in Parisian and in diplomatic circles.'[11] Writing of Eddy's official functions, he was equally complimentary: 'I have always found him most ready to be of use in any direction, and I am indebted to him for assiduity in furnishing me with information of importance which otherwise might never have reached me.'[12]

On the question of the advisability of a visit to Paris by the King, however, the Ambassador and the Military Attaché differed: Sir Edmund was against it and Eddy for it.[13] But Edward VII made up his mind to visit Lisbon, Rome and Paris in State in the spring of 1903, and he proceeded without the advice of his ministers; indeed, neither Lord Knollys, his Private Secretary, nor the Queen knew what he had in mind until his plans had been made. Instead of the Foreign Secretary, he turned first to the Marquis de Soveral, the Portuguese Minister in London, who had become a friend, and it was he who arranged the visit to Lisbon, with the King of Portugal.

It seems to be the case that it was de Soveral, too, who arranged the visit to Paris, with the President of the Republic, M. Loubert; Monson was not consulted, but a go-between was needed, and this was evidently Eddy, who is said to have been close to the President.[14] 'In order to ensure privacy', wrote one of the King's biographers, Giles St. Aubyn, 'communications from London were sent to the Colonel's house in the Rue de la Faisanderie. Stuart Wortley's wife was never told from whom these secret letters came, but she suspected that they were written either by the King or de Soveral.'[15] Unfortunately, some of the King's papers were destroyed after his death, and the Royal Archives now contain no evidence of all this.[16]

The King left Rome for Paris on 30th April, and Monson joined his special train at Dijon on the morning of 1st May. He was welcomed to Paris by President Loubet, who drove with him in a splendid procession along the Champs Elysées to the British Embassy. The crowds were by no means entirely friendly, but Edward was not put out: 'As always he appeared to exude warmth and friendliness, and every movement and gesture which he made was stamped with a calculated and inimitable geniality developed to the pitch of a fine art.'[17] He paid a visit to the President at the Elysée, and afterwards, at the Embassy, he received a deputation from the British Chamber of Commerce in Paris. He then delivered a speech to the deputation, so worded in its references to France that reports of it began to change popular opinion of him.

That evening, the process of change in popular opinion continued at the theatre. He was received with indifference if not hostility; during an interval, however, he joined some of the audience in the foyer and noticed a certain well-known actress, his gallantry towards whom delighted everyone. The next day, it was the same story; at a military review at Vincenne, a reception at the Hôtel de Ville and a race meeting at Longchamps, all held in his honour, his charm and courtesy prevailed; a lunch for old friends at the Embassy posed no problems. Crowds along his route to Vincenne and Longchamps greeted him noticeably more warmly than those on the Champs Elysées, though still with some reserve.

The high point of the visit was reached on the second evening, when there was a state banquet at the Elysée and a gala performance at the Opera. The King spoke particularly warmly at the banquet, and word spread to the streets. When he came out, he was greeted with feeling: the people began chanting 'Vive le Roi!', 'Vive Edouard!', 'Notre bon Edouard!' and French variants of 'Good old Teddy!';[18] and his carriage had difficulty in making its way through the crowds to the Opera. At the Opera, too, he was fêted. He was not to return to London until 4$^{th}$ May, so that he had another full day of engagements to which to look forward, but he must have been satisfied that evening that the visit was a success.

The King made a number of appointments to the Royal Victorian Order on this visit, as he did on other foreign visits. The French Prime Minister, the French Foreign Minister, the French Ambassador in London and others were made honorary Knights Grand Cross of the Order;[19] Eddy and others were made Members. When the time came for Eddy to leave Paris, the President was flattering, but there was nothing about his final audience, at least as Eddy reported it, to support the view that they had been close. 'The President was most cordial in his reception', Eddy told Monson, 'and was kind enough to say that he had been informed by the military members of his staff how much my departure was regretted.'[20]

# CHAPTER ELEVEN

## HALF PAY

THERE WAS no new post for Eddy until the spring of 1908: he was on half-pay for four years; which cannot have been easy for him, because he was not a wealthy man, and the Highcliffe estate was as much a liability as an asset.[1] This explains why the Castle was let for long periods; as it probably was in 1904 and 1905, since there are no entries in the Visitors' Book for those two years.[2] There were various smaller houses in the neighbourhood of which the family could make use, occasionally if not regularly: they had no town house; it must have been at about this time, however, that Eddy acquired rooms in Clarges Street, off Piccadilly,[3] and it may have been at the same time that he became a member of two London clubs, the Turf and Boodles.[4]

The Stuart Wortleys returned from Paris in July 1904, and they spent the rest of that summer on the island of Mull, in a house on the estate of Violet's brother, Murray.[5] Scottish blood flowed strongly in the veins of both Violet and Eddy, and Violet thought the place romantic; we do not know what Eddy thought of it, but we do know that grand friends whom they invited to stay obviously had no idea what they were letting themselves in for. It must be remembered that it was a century ago. 'I had been rash enough to invite some friends from abroad,' said Violet, 'and witnessed their utter dismay at what they considered primitive existence.'[6] Fortunately, the party was cheered by the arrival on the island of Murray and a large party of his own, and then by the arrival off the island of Admiral Lord Charles Beresford and a squadron of warships.

The next recorded episode in Eddy's life was the visit to Highcliffe of the young King Alfonso XIII of Spain on 27$^{th}$ April, 1906.[7] This was an outing from Osborne House, on the Isle of Wight, like such outings in the days of Queen Victoria and Lady Waterford. It is said that Alfonso was courting Princess Ena of Battenberg, and that she had a cold and had to be left behind; there was a large enough party of foreign royalty, with their aides, and English courtiers, all the same. They were shown the Castle, with Lord Stuart de Rothesay's library and his collections, and given lunch; and then Alfonso planted a commemorative tree. Violet said in her autobiography that the tree died, for no apparent reason, shortly after Alfonso abdicated in 1931, though she made no other comment on what she called 'this horticultural phenomenon'.[8]

Alfonso XIII was born King of Spain, in 1886, his father, Alfonso XII, having died during the pregnancy of his wife, Queen Maria Christina. He married Princess Victoria Eugenia, daughter of Prince Henry of Battenberg. He reigned in troubled times for Spain, but the country had a troubled history, in one episode of which Lord Stuart de Rothesay figured.[9] He made himself unpopular, by lending legitimacy to the dictatorship of Primo de Rivera, for instance, and in 1931 he was obliged to flee the country. Many years later, Violet met him in exile in Rome. 'He recalled his visit to Highcliffe with a warm eagerness,' she said, 'recollecting happier days.'[10] It is unlikely that Eddy ever saw him again.

Nellie Melba made the first of many visits to Highcliffe at the end of that year, on 16th December, 1906.[11] The Stuart Wortleys had met her when she had come to Paris, to sing at a benefit concert for her teacher Mme Mathilde Marchesi,[12] and they had become friends. The prima donna was born Helen Porter Mitchell, in 1861, in Melbourne, where she was also trained; but she studied later in London and Paris, and then adopted her professional name. Her voice was described as 'extraordinarily fresh and beautiful, with power and expansion and perfectly even through two and a half octaves',[13] and she sang in many of the capitals of the world between 1886 and 1926. It was only in 1918 that she was appointed DBE and became Dame Nellie.

Until this unwelcome interlude in his career, Eddy had spent little time at Highcliffe: now he had an opportunity to make himself at home. Records of his activities are thin: the Highcliffe parish magazine is an otherwise useful source of information about local events, but there is a gap in the series here; and a strong family link between the Castle and the church makes this particularly disappointing. Eddy was Patron of the Living of Highcliffe, and his predecessors at the Castle had been, and as such had the right of nomination when a new vicar was needed for the parish, though only the bishop could make the appointment. At the end of this interlude, the Reverend Stanley Carpenter left Highcliffe and Eddy nominated the Reverend Frederick Gray, who was duly appointed by the Bishop of Winchester.

Meanwhile, significant changes were taking place in the affairs of the British Army. The Boer War had shown up, only too clearly, the inadequacies of the Army's organisation, and in 1904 and 1905, under the Conservative Government of Arthur Balfour, reform began. In 1904 the Army Council was set up, to provide the Secretary for War with a better source of advice than was represented by the out-dated office of Commander-in-Chief of the British Army, which was abolished. In 1905 there followed the even more important Committee of Imperial Defence, the function of which was to collect and collate information, and provide appropriate advice concerning all aspects of the defence of Great Britain and what was then the British Empire.

Richard Burdon Haldane, Secretary for War in the Liberal Government of Sir Henry Campbell-Bannerman, carried out a more thoroughgoing scheme of reform, beginning in 1907. He was responsible for the creation of a General Staff, the existence of which during the Boer War might have prevented a number of gaffes; an Expeditionary Force, in effect a complete army ready for rapid mobilisation; and a unified Territorial Force, which was to loom large at the end of Eddy's career. 'Possessing a special knowledge of German institutions', one historian has written of Haldane, 'he brought it to bear with far-reaching effects on the War

Office.'[14] Ironically, his possession of this special knowledge was regarded with suspicion and held against him when war broke out in 1914.

When Eddy's obituary came to be written for his regimental journal, attention was paid to the fact that his early promise was never realised, and the obituarist posited a link with these reforms.

> He was so full of the *joie de vivre* that he simply cannot have found time to make a serious study of his profession, and so, during the years after the South African War, when the British Army took seriously to soldiering, he remained something of an amateur.[15]

Be that as it may, he reached the substantive rank of colonel on 23$^{rd}$ February, 1907.[16]

But one of the most extraordinary events of Eddy's life and career, if not the most extraordinary, took place during that period, in which he might have considered himself to be marking time. This was the visit to Highcliffe of the Kaiser, William II, of Germany.

# CHAPTER TWELVE

## THE KAISER AT HIGHCLIFFE

THE KAISER, William II, spent three weeks at Highcliffe Castle, after his State visit with the Kaiserin to King Edward VII and Queen Alexandra at Windsor, in 1907. The Stuart Wortleys did not have much warning: it was in a letter dated 8th November, written on behalf of Sir Edward Grey, the Foreign Secretary, that they were asked if they would let the Castle for his use, with everything in it, including servants;[1] it was on 18th November that he arrived with his suite, though without the Kaiserin, who had returned to Berlin. The reply to Sir Edward has been lost, but an endorsement to his letter shows that the house was lent on condition that Eddy remained as the Kaiser's host; and this endorsement shows, too, that Highcliffe had been recommended by the King, who knew the place well.

It says much for the Stuart Wortleys' organisational skills that all the necessary plans and preparations were made in time. Unfortunately, the Castle had already been let to Sir Alfred Cooper, the surgeon, and his wife, and they had to be persuaded to move, with all their baggage and servants, into a house that happened to be available nearby. Eddy and Violet had moved out sometime earlier, in readiness for this letting, but accommodation in the village had also to be found for the numerous suite. Catering might have been a problem, but the King had thought of this, and Mrs Rosa Lewis, of the Cavendish Hotel in Jermyn Street, had agreed to take over the kitchen. The King had once known the Cavendish Hotel better than he knew Highcliffe.

Rosa Lewis was no ordinary cook and no ordinary woman: her experience of life had left her equipped to hold her own in any company. The Kaiser wanted nothing to do with anything or any one French, but she was Francophile, and it was said of her at

**Kaiser Willhelm II**
By Philip de Laszlo
By courtesy of the Witt Library, Courtauld Institute, London.

Highcliffe that 'she did not believe in spoiling the artistic *toute ensemble* of the dinners she prepared by pandering to imperial prejudices.'[2] French dishes were served and there were no complaints. Indeed, William was full of compliments; when he left Highcliffe, he gave her a hundred pounds, a decoration, a signed print of his portrait by Laszlo and a brooch.[3] When war came, she returned the decoration and hung the portrait in a lavatory but kept the brooch.[4]

It was said that William fancied himself to be living the life of an English country gentleman, but the imperial appurtenances were there for all to see. There was his retinue, the size of which, according to Violet, had horrified the King;[5] though it must be said that some of the gentlemen had returned to Berlin with the Kaiserin. There was the special train, used by the ministers who came and went, and by Rosa Lewis, who did most of her shopping in London. There was also the royal yacht, the *Hohenzollern*, lying in Christchurch Bay, from which the band would come ashore in the evening to serenade His Majesty and any guests that he might have. Less obvious was the post office, in the Castle's basement, set up to deal with letters and telegrams and telephone calls.

He was on holiday. 'He seemed to forget for a while the heavy responsibility that rested on his shoulders,' said Violet. 'Seldom before he had been so untrammelled by the laws of etiquette, and the cast-iron system of the Prussian Court. I felt that his spirits were like those of a schoolboy released from school.'[6] He began the day in spartan mode, however, with a cold bath of sea water, brought to his room before 8 o'clock, and there was usually business to be done, with ministers and officials, after breakfast; but the afternoon was for visiting and sightseeing. A fleet of cars would be assembled in front of the Castle and, accompanied by Eddy, he and a party from his suite would drive off into the country.

He visited several of the neighbouring country houses, at each of which he was entertained informally and shown its treasures. A photograph of his party, now hanging unobtrusively in a bedroom,

**The Kaiser with his entourage and Edward Stuart Wortley at Highcliffe Castle in 1907**

Photograph by courtesy of Ian Stevenson

and a terracotta bust in the library, commemorate his visit to Kingston Lacy. Churches interested him as much as the country houses, and he is known to have visited Christchurch Priory and Romsey Abbey. The feedback to Violet was that he was knowledgeable on the subject of architecture and obviously well read in history, and that he had corrected the Vicar of Romsey on a matter of dates. Violet seems to have liked him, even later, but she was to remark, tartly, in one of her books that his reading about the past did not save him from making 'one of the worst blunders in history'.[7]

On the first Sunday of his visit to Highcliffe he attended matins at the parish church. He is likely to have been gratified by a sermon preached on the work of the Universities' Mission to Central Africa, since the mission was supported by the German Government, though he mentioned almost everything except that in the message of thanks that he sent to the Vicar afterwards.[8] 'He had been discouraged from reading the lesson in Highcliffe Church', Violet wrote, in satirical vein, 'but he had joined loudly in singing the hymns'.[9] Another Sunday saw him at Christchurch Priory. 'Meekly, he seemed to suffer the Vicar of Christchurch to preach to him', Violet wrote of this occasion, 'while he appeared to convey that really it would have been more seemly if he himself had been invited to occupy the pulpit'.[10]

One account, not too far from the event, has it that 'a walk to the village was something the Kaiser thoroughly enjoyed'.[11] There is no mention of a retinue or the reaction of the villagers. 'Often, in the course of it,' this account goes on, referring to such a promenade, 'he entered shops to chat with whoever might be there, or to buy sweets for a village boy or girl.' Sometimes he would walk in the other direction: there was at least one occasion on which Eddy accompanied him along what was then a country lane that led to Mudeford; and since they were discussing high politics, and the Kaiser was being indiscreet about Japan, the retinue may have been left behind.[12] On this occasion they dropped in on one of the Stuart Wortleys' neighbours.[13]

The most memorable event of those three weeks for the children of Highcliffe was undoubtedly the tea party that William gave for them, on 30$^{th}$ November, in the schoolroom.[14] They were able to make the most of it, whether by accident or design, before he arrived, and they were evidently not unduly inhibited by his presence. Formalities were observed: he was received by the Vicar, with whom he 'took tea', he was presented with two baskets of flowers by two little girls and he cut the cake, which was three feet high; but he walked about the room, too, more or less informally, making himself pleasant to the children and the helpers. He did not stay long, and when he left the children cheered him.

Though Eddy was acting as the Kaiser's host, he had not been able to stay at the Castle, and he was living for the time being at Nea Farm,[15] on the outskirts of the village. Violet, with Louise and Bettine, was away, probably staying with her sister, Lady Rodd, in London;[16] Rothesay was at school. Violet and the two girls were there, with Eddy, when William planted a commemorative tree in the Castle grounds, however, and she was invited to dinner at the Castle on his last night at Highcliffe. That evening, Violet was to recall, he spoke 'rather freely' about German affairs.[17] From Highcliffe, William returned to London; but when he left for Berlin Eddy and Violet were among the party that saw him off from Charing Cross.

# CHAPTER THIRTEEN

## THE *DAILY TELEGRAPH* 'INTERVIEW'

ON 28th OCTOBER, 1908, the *Daily Telegraph* published what purported to be an interview with the Kaiser by an anonymous retired diplomat.[1] Its object was said to be an improvement in relations between England and Germany, but there was much about it that was foolish and indiscreet, and it caused offence in both those countries and in others too. So serious were its repercussions in Germany that the Kaiser talked of abdication and his chief minister, the Imperial Chancellor, Prince Bülow, eventually resigned. The retired diplomat was Eddy, who had had diplomatic status, after all, as a military attaché; the so-called interview was, in effect, a summary of discussions that had taken place at Highcliffe in 1907 and in Germany earlier in 1908.

At Highcliffe in 1907, Eddy was given several opportunities of discussing the issues of the day with His Majesty, in private: fortunately, he recorded what was said straightaway, in the form of letters to Violet, of which there are three in the records.[2] Then, in return for his hospitality at Highcliffe, Eddy was invited to attend the manoeuvres of the German Army in 1908. There is some disagreement in the available records as to the duration of Eddy's visit and the time he spent with the Kaiser: Violet said he spent 'several weeks with the Imperial Headquarters Staff looking on at the German Army engaged in training operations',[3] and that there were 'long talks with the Kaiser himself';[4] a letter to Eddy from one of William's staff, dated 14th June, gave the dates of the then forthcoming manoeuvres as 8th - 10th September.[5]

Eddy's own account was published in the form of a letter to the *Daily Telegraph* in 1930.

> In the autumn of 1908 I received an invitation to attend the German manoeuvres at Saarbrucken as the Kaiser's guest. On the concluding day of the manoeuvres the Emperor sent for me. He was on his horse in the middle of a ploughed field. He told his staff to clear away for some distance, and proceeded to recount to me all that eventually appeared in the interview which was published. He concluded by saying he wished me to use my discretion and to have the gist of the interview published in a leading English newspaper.[6]

It is surprising that Eddy did not mention the discussions at Highcliffe. Assuming that his memory of events was reliable, however, it is interesting to note that it was the Kaiser who took the initiative in having the 'interview' published.

But Eddy was not slow to follow up the initiative: the necessary arrangements had been made by 23rd September,[7] through a friend in Fleet Street, Harry Lawson, son of the proprietor of the *Daily Telegraph*, Lord Burnham; all that was then needed was the Kaiser's approval. Again, we have Eddy's own account of all this in the letter already quoted.

> In accordance with my request that a member of the *Daily Telegraph* staff should be sent to take down at my dictation an account of the interview, Mr J.B. Firth came to my rooms at Clarges Street and took down word for word all I had to relate. The account of the interview was then typewritten and returned to me. I forwarded it under seal, through the German Embassy, direct to the Emperor, asking him to say whether he considered it an accurate account of what he had told me.[8]

The typescript, embossed with the newspaper's title, is preserved in the records.[9]

Eddy's letter to the Kaiser, accompanying the typescript, made his personal feelings clear: 'I am only one of Your Majesty's great admirers in this country, whose great wish it is to prove to the people of England Your Majesty's firm desire to be on the best of terms with them.'[10] He went on, however, to draw William's attention to the importance to him of anonymity. Official disapproval of his part in the affair would have fallen heavily on him as a serving officer, by this time a brigadier-general. 'As I am but a humble soldier,' he explained, 'I must respectfully ask Your Majesty that this matter may be kept absolutely confidential.'

Exactly what happened to the draft in Germany is not clear: there are several versions of the story. Both the Kaiser and the Chancellor, Prince Bülow were away from Berlin, and the Foreign Minister, William von Schoen was away from the Foreign Office; which may help to explain the mistakes that were made; but Bülow was finally responsible for the advice that was given to the Kaiser. When William received the document from Eddy he sent it to Bülow, for his opinion on it, as he was bound to do, and Bülow delegated responsibility for its scrutiny to the Foreign Office. William eventually received it back with three minor alterations, in the form of marginal notes, and the advice that there was no reason why it should not be published.

The document was returned to Eddy in the state in which it had been returned to William, accompanied by a personal letter. This letter was hand written, though apparently not by William, who signed it himself nevertheless.

    Confidentially

    Neus Palais

                             October 15$^{th}$ 1908

    Dear Colonel (sic) Stuart Wortley,

    I have carefully examined the draft of a communiqué to the press which you kindly sent me with your letter of September 23$^{rd}$ and which I treated, as you desired, most confidentially. It embodied correctly all the principal items of our conversation during the recent manoeuvres and deals in a most reasonable and straightforward manner with the justified complaints which I have to make against certain organs of the English press. In three places only, on pages 3, 4 and 7, I propose some small alterations in the wording of the draft. With these alterations which are noted in the margin, I authorise you to make a discrete (sic) use of the article in the manner you think best. I firmly hope that it may have the affect of bringing about a change in the tone of some of the English newspapers.

Thanking you most sincerely for the endeavours you have been taking in the matter, believe me, dear Colonel Stuart Wortley,

Yours very truly,

William IR [11]

The article that caused the trouble consists of about two thousand words and takes up nearly two columns of the newspaper, under four headlines of diminishing size of print: 'The German Emperor and England'; 'Personal Interview'; 'Frank Statement of World Policy'; and 'Proofs of Friendship'. There is a brief introduction by one of the editorial staff of the paper, and this is followed by a long apologia from Eddy, in his character of diplomat. His indiscretion in making public what the Kaiser had said to him in private is justified, he maintains, tongue in cheek, by the chance that it gives him of removing, or helping to remove, the prejudice against His Majesty that exists in the minds of many Englishmen. Throughout, references are to England rather than Great Britain.

The so-called interview, itself, begins with a section in which the Kaiser is critical of England's failure to respond to his overtures of friendship. 'I have said time after time that I am a friend of England,' he is quoted as saying, in a particular purple patch, 'and your Press – or at least, a considerable section of it – bids the people of England refuse my proffered hand, and intimates that the other holds a dagger.' It was bad enough for many of his people that he should profess himself an Anglophile, but he went on to make matters worse by claiming that what he called 'the best elements' of German society shared his feelings: those who did not happen to share his feelings resented the implied slur.

Next, Eddy raised the subject of Germany's interest in Morocco, which was causing concern. The Sultan had been deposed, and the European Powers had agreed not to recognise the new regime until certain assurances as to its intentions were forthcoming. All consular officials had left the capital during the crisis but the German consul had already returned, and the inference was that Germany had double-crossed the other Powers. At this point in the draft, one of the alterations occurs. According to the draft, the Kaiser stated that the consul had returned 'entirely on his own account;' the published version has it that, in Germany's view, the required assurances had been as good as given. The alteration must have given those who were aware of it food for thought.

Then the Kaiser reverted to his central theme: his friendship for England; and he used the Boer War to illustrate it. When a party of Boers was touring Europe, drumming up support for their cause, he said, he had refused to receive them, and his refusal had had a salutary effect on public opinion. Whatever may have been the truth of this, however, it paled into insignificance beside his next claim, which was that France and Russia had invited Germany to join them in forcing England to make peace with the Boers, in order not merely to save the Boer republics but also to humiliate England, and that he had rejected the very idea. Reaction in Paris and St. Petersburg was restrained, but it soon became known that the boot was on the other foot.[12]

'Nor was that all,' William went on. He had advised the English military authorities on their conduct of the war. At a dark moment in the conflict, he said, he had received a letter from his 'revered grandmother', Queen Victoria, expressing her fears and anxieties; he had responded with a plan of campaign, based on information from the German military authorities but drawn up by himself. Whether or not this plan was of use, the fact was, he maintained, that the plan followed by Lord Roberts bore a close resemblance to it. Boer sympathisers in Germany were staggered, but there was more amusement than anger in England. Laughter greeted a statement to the House of Commons, that searches of the relevant archives had failed to reveal the document to which His Majesty referred.[13]

Last but not least came a section devoted to the German Navy. There had been a great increase in German naval power in recent years, and it was an open secret that the object of this was to challenge the Royal Navy for supremacy at sea. William claimed, however, that Germany was concerned only with the protection of her commercial interests worldwide, and with the anticipation of problems in the Far East. 'Look at the established rise of Japan,' he urged; 'think of the possible national awakening of China.' Japan was bemused,[14] and *The Times* wanted an explanation for the presence of large numbers of German warships in the North Sea and the Baltic. Many of these ships, the newspaper pointed out, lacked the fuel capacity for long cruises.[15]

The reaction to the article came first from the press, in England and Germany and other countries: in England, it was largely sceptical and dismissive, though there was anger at the offence given to Lord Roberts; in Germany, there was almost universal condemnation, even newspapers on which the Kaiser could usually rely for support joining in the chorus of disapproval.[16] All this was as nothing, however, to the reaction in the German parliament, the Reichstag. Here, during a long debate, there were what the British Ambassador at Berlin, Sir Edward Goschen, described as violent attacks on both the Kaiser and the Chancellor;[17] and Bülow's contribution did nothing to improve his position.

Bülow's position had been weak from the first, since the responsibility for what had occurred could reasonably be said to be his. Later, in his memoirs, he published his own account of the affair, which included the text of a report that he submitted to the Kaiser. In the report, he offered the excuse that he had been too busy to read the document himself;[18] but this does not seem good enough, since what was under consideration was the draft of an article to be published in the name of the Kaiser, and nobody knew better than Bülow that His Majesty was gaffe-prone. Hoping to explain the difficulty in which he had found himself more fully, he described the draft as 'written almost illegibly on bad paper':[19] the evidence is that what he was shown was typewritten and perfectly legible.

But though the affair marked the beginning of the end of Bülow's chancellorship, it had a more devastating effect on the Kaiser. He went through what he called a period of 'great mental anguish'[20], which some historians have ranked as a mental breakdown;[21&22] it was then that he talked of abdication. His depression, if that is what it was, soon lifted, but he was never the same again. Whatever his true feelings and intentions, his attempt to establish friendly relations between Germany and England, or at least between himself and the English people, had only made matters worse; and he had lost standing in the eyes of the world.

The British Foreign Secretary, Sir Edward Grey, summed up the situation for himself in a letter to a colleague, from London on 26th November.

> Never since I have been in office has opinion here been so thoroughly wide awake with regard to Germany, and on its guard as it is now. I haven't the faintest tremor of doubt about that. Never has the Emperor's position been so low in the world.[23]

Eddy must have been badly shaken. Before the full extent of the debacle had unfolded, on 31st October, he wrote to the Kaiser to share his distress.[24] 'I cannot say how disappointed and miserable I feel', he wrote. But he thought he knew who to blame for what had gone wrong. 'It is more than lamentable,' he went on, 'that journalists should be so steeped in the mire of deceipt (sic) and intrigue, that it can become almost foreign to them to recognise that anyone can be straightforward ...' Perhaps other letters followed, and perhaps they were answered, as the situation went from bad to worse during the weeks that followed, but neither originals nor copies have come to light.

Eddy remained on good terms with the Kaiser, at least until war came: we do not know what his feelings were then. He had misjudged William, and he may have been naïve to have done so, but he cannot be blamed for having taken the opportunity, with which he had been so fortuitously presented, as he saw it, to promote peace in Europe. Either he did not see what others saw in William's character or he discounted it, and since he referred to him as a 'straightforward' man he evidently did not see it: William was an unstable man and his power made him all the more dangerous. G.M. Treveylan put it neatly: 'The Kaiser had the artist's temperament that would have flourished in the Quartier Latin, but was warped by Byzantine pomp and power'.[25]

# CHAPTER FOURTEEN

## SHORNCLIFFE

FROM 28th APRIL, 1908 to 27th APRIL, 1912, Eddy commanded the 10th Infantry Brigade at Shorncliffe Camp, near Folkestone, with the rank of brigadier-general. The camp had particular historical associations, which, as it happened, meant as much to Eddy as to any previous commandant, if not more. Sir Basil Liddell Hart wrote of it:

> For any solider with a sense of history Shorncliffe was an inspiring spot, for here Sir John Moore had conducted the most important of earlier experiments in developing new tactical methods for the British Army, when training the famous Light Brigade preparatory to the fight with Napoleon's armies in the Peninsular War.[1]

Sir John Moore worked closely in the Peninsula with the young diplomat Charles Stuart, later to become Lord Stuart de Rothesay: he had served in Corsica under that Charles Stuart's father, General Sir Charles Stuart, whom he had greatly admired.[2]

The centenary of Moore's death, at Corunna, on 16th January, 1809, fell during Eddy's period of command, and it was marked locally and nationally. Later in 1909, a monument was erected at Sandgate, on the edge of the sea, below the camp: it was a granite obelisk, with his sculped bust in bas-relief and an inscription recording the grounds of his fame; a form of memorial that seems particularly appropriate in the light of Charles Wolfe's famous lines on his hurried burial, to the sound of French gunfire.

> We carved not a line, and raised not a stone –
> But we left him alone with his glory.[3]

It was unveiled by Moore's great niece, Miss Mary Carrick-Moore.

This was a routine peacetime appointment for Eddy, and as such it did not attract the sort of attention that makes for interesting records. The local newspapers of the period regularly published items about the camp, however, and some of these include references to Eddy. From a scrap book of cuttings we learn, for instance, that a new hospital at the camp was opened by Princess Christian of Schleswig-Holstein, Queen Victoria's daughter, in 1909; that 'a portable cooking apparatus' invented by Eddy was given a trial during military exercises in 1910; and that a charity concert arranged by Eddy and Violet in 1912 was a great success.[4] Violet was presented to Princess Christian, and must have remembered the occasion later, when she shared war work with the Princess's daughter, Princess Helena Victoria.

Because it was a routine peacetime appointment, Eddy was able to have his family with him. Violet played the part no doubt expected of the commandant's wife in the life of the camp and the local community, but Rothesay was at Oxford and Louise and Bettine were at school, for some time in Brussels.[5] For Violet, one of the most memorable events of their time at Shorncliffe was the charity concert.[6] It was a public event, held in a Folkestone theatre; and though local papers would have been unlikely to be anything but polite about such an occasion, it is not surprising to read that it 'drew a crowded audience'.[7] Nellie Melba, by now a friend, was one of the attractions, and she had persuaded other well-known artistes to appear.

An equally memorable event must surely have been what a reporter on one of the papers called a bear's 'bold bid for freedom' from captivity at the camp. Memorable as this must have been, there are certain discrepancies between Violet's version of the story, published forty years later,[8] and the report in the paper at the time;[9] though these are unimportant. Violet's version is prefaced by another story that must be told first. David Lloyd George, then Chancellor of the Exchequer, used sometimes to stay with friends in the neighbourhood, and on one of his visits he surprised Eddy with a formal invitation to a badger hunt. Eddy replied, equally formally, accepting the invitation, and was apparently greatly entertained by the unusual proceedings.

The bear had been brought back from India by a returning regiment as a pet, but it had not taken kindly to domesticity or captivity. It escaped soon after Lloyd George's badger hunt, and Eddy was not slow to take advantage of the coincidence: in the most formal terms, he invited the Chancellor of the Exchequer to a bear hunt. 'The great man appreciated the humour and turned out suitably equipped,' said Violet, without describing the equipment. Again according to Violet, the entire brigade turned out with Eddy and Lloyd George, and town and country were scoured all day without success; but when the men returned to their quarters they found the animal, in a somnolent and tractable state, close to it where it had last been seen.

The public was sometimes invited to the camp. There is an announcement in the *Folkestone Herald* of 31st October, 1908, for instance, of a meeting to be held there on 9th November. This was to celebrate the golden jubilee of the Papillion Soldiers' Home, a forerunner of the NAAFI and said to be the oldest of such amenities. Eddy was to take the chair, and there were to be talks on the history and the work of the Home. A band was to play during the afternoon; donations were invited to a building fund. The dates are worth noting, since the *Daily Telegraph* 'interview' appeared on 28th October, and by 9th November Eddy is likely to have found it difficult to concentrate on his duties at Shorncliffe.

Eddy had had leave to attend the manoeuvres of the German Army in the autumn of 1908, but was not as free to travel while he was at Shorncliffe as he was to be later. Violet, on the other hand, made several trips abroad during this time. Her brother-in-law, Sir Rennell Rodd, was Ambassador at Rome; he and his wife, Violet's sister Lilias, had a villa with a private beach outside Naples, and she, Rothesay, Louise and Bettine stayed with them and their children there. On another occasion, she took Rothesay and Louise to Dublin, to stay with Eddy's relations the Lytteltons, 'for a week of festivities which would include a ball at the Castle and Punchestown Races'.[10] General Lyttelton had become General Sir Neville Lyttelton, Commander-in-Chief of the Army in Ireland.

Between this and his next appointment, Eddy had time both to travel and to enjoy Highcliffe. Within this brief stretch of time, on 9th January, 1913, fell Rothesay's twenty-first birthday, which was celebrated in due form. Looking back on the party half a century later, however, Violet felt nothing but sadness. 'How could we know', she wrote of Rothesay and his friends, 'that almost while their laughter was still ringing in our ears, the First World War would burst out, and that the happy insouciance of those gay Edwardian days would vanish, never to return'.[11]

**Major-General The Honourable Edward Stuart Wortley**
With acknowledgements to The Bodleian Library, University of Oxford.
Reference: 22281 e 160.

# CHAPTER FIFTEEN

## THE GREAT WAR (1)

OVER A PERIOD of twenty years, from 1894, there was a build-up of German military and naval capability: in the face of this, step by step, France and Russia, Britain and France, and finally, Britain and Russia made alliances. Germany reacted to what was seen from Berlin as encirclement by establishing a close relationship with Austria, but the relationship between Austria and Russia was strained by rival claims in the Balkans, and the assassination of the Austrian Archduke Franz Ferdinand at Sarajevo on 28$^{th}$ June, 1914, was the spark that set the fire. Austria asked for the support of Germany in exacting reparations from Serbia, and was given what has been described as a blank cheque.[1] Britain declared war when Germany invaded Belgium; the great issue, however, was the balance of power in Europe.

When the war began, on 4$^{th}$ August, 1914, Eddy was in command of the North Midland Territorial Division. The Division was based at Derby, and Violet hastened from Highcliffe to join her husband; her gesture would have been more impressive if she had not chosen to stay with the Duchess of Devonshire at Chatsworth,[2] but it is only fair to add that Chatsworth was already being placed on a war footing. Gone already were the days, fondly remembered by Violet, when hospitality at the great houses was dispensed on such a scale that the Duchess, herself, sometimes lost count of her guests.[3] Soon the Division was moved to Bedfordshire, and training began in earnest: it was no secret that Eddy wanted the North Midland to be the first territorial division to be sent to France.[4]

It was said that Eddy spent much time at the War Office asking for embarkation orders,[5] and whether or not on account of his importunity the North Midland was, in fact, the first territorial division to be sent to France. King George V inspected the Division

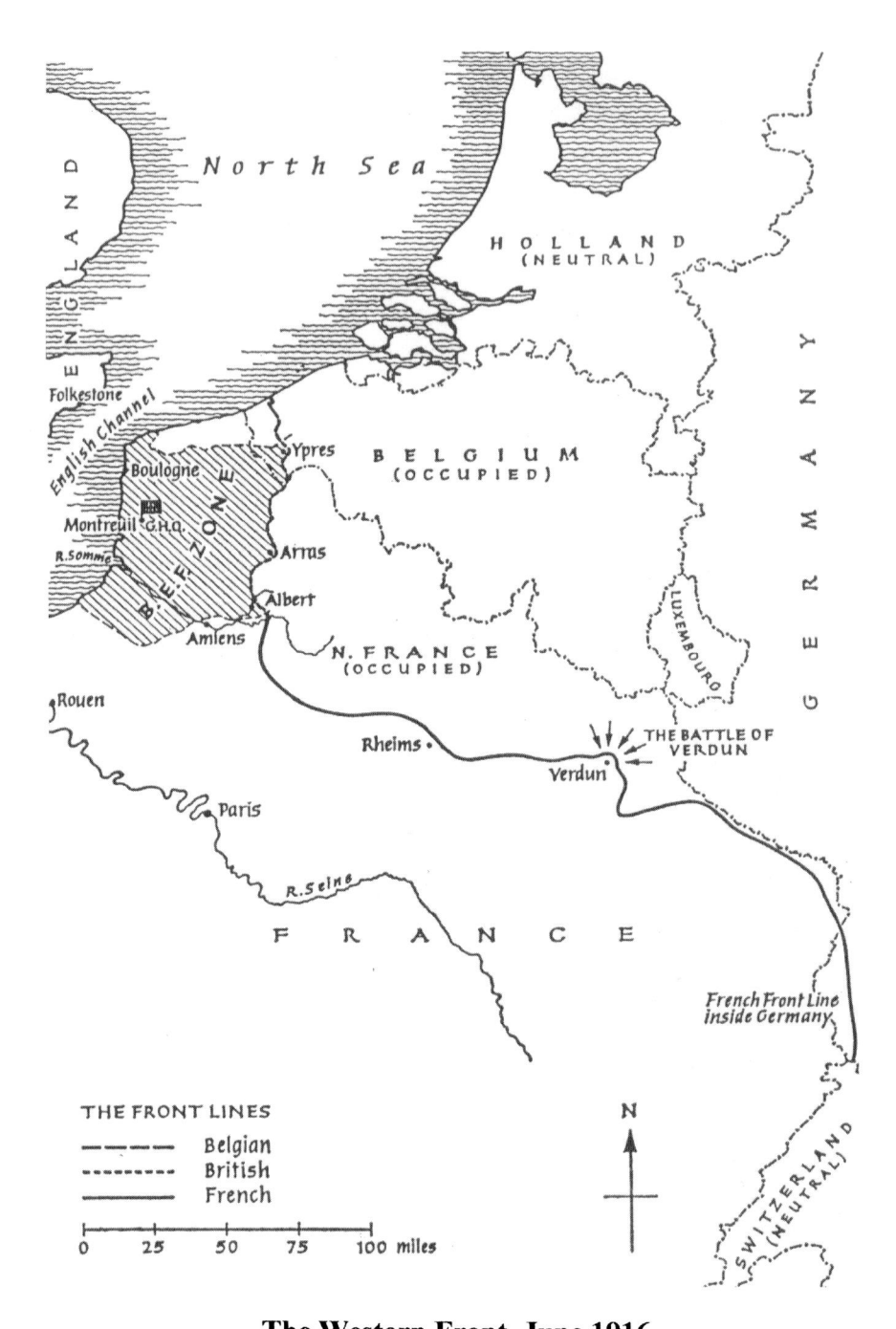

**The Western Front, June 1916**
From: *The First Day of The Somme*, by Martin Middlebrook

before it left England, and he made a request of Eddy then that, as will be seen, had unfortunate consequences for him: he asked him to write to him every week. A request from the King was a command; nevertheless, Eddy had the sense to ask permission of the Commander-in-Chief in France, Sir John French, and of his more immediate superior, Sir Horace Smith-Dorrien, before he began to write, and he ceased to write when, as he put it, he could not continue 'without treading on the dangerous ground of criticism'.[6]

The North Midland Division was made up of men from Leicestershire, Lincolnshire, Nottinghamshire and Staffordshire. It was part of the Territorial Force, later to be called the Territorial Army, which had been formed in 1907 by the amalgamation of various regionally-based volunteer forces, such as the militia, to become a reserve as well as a home defence force. The Division joined the British Expeditionary Force in France in February 1915, and then became the 46th (North Midland) Division: Eddy, at about this time, was described as 'tall, lanky, stooping slightly, red-faced, moustached, immaculately dressed, brass-hatted, with medal ribbons in rows', and it was said that he addressed his men always in the same 'easy drawling voice'.[7]

The 46th (North Midland) Division was present at the Battle of Neuve Chapelle, 10th - 13th March, but was held on reserve. Neuve Chapelle lay between the two major British war zones of the Western Front, the Ypres Salient and the Somme: it was part of the German defences of Aubers Ridge, important strategically for its dominating position; and beyond Aubers Ridge lay the town of Lille, even more important strategically for its industry and railway junction. General Sir Douglas Haig was in command, and when he stopped the fighting little had been gained in terms of ground and much had been lost in terms of casualties. Haig's tactics, particularly his repeated frontal attacks, were much criticised.[8]

In the summer of 1915, the Division is said to have 'held a dangerous part of the Ypres Salient with many casualties but no chance for glory'.[9] On 19th July, 30th July and 9th August, however,

**Field Marshal Sir John French**
Later Earl of Ypres
By John Singer Sargent RA
By courtesy of the National Portrait Gallery, London.

the North Midlanders took part in a series of fierce engagements at Hooge that brought them credit if not glory.[10] On 19th July, a large crater was made on the German side of the line, by means of a tunnel and a mine, taking the enemy by surprise, and this super-trench was immediately occupied, while German positions to right and left were also attacked. The Germans counter-attacked on 30th July, using flame-throwers for the first time, and much of the ground that had been gained was lost. The next move was planned and prepared with great care, and on 9th August a small victory was won.

The Battle of Loos, 25th September – 4th November, was planned, in conjunction with a French offensive in Champagne, to relieve the Russians of German pressure on the Eastern Front; it was fought not far from Neuve Chapelle, and as at Neuve Chapelle losses were out of all proportion to gains. 'For the British, Loos was a setback that caused much heart-searching and distress. Of nearly 10,000 British soldiers who attacked at Loos, 385 officers and 7,861 men were killed or wounded.'[11] Self-deception was swept away in England, in the most loyal and patriotic quarters; both Neuve Chapelle and Loos began to be talked of as defeats,[12] and it was not long before Sir John French, who had been responsible for the overall direction of the battle, was replaced as Commander-in-Chief in France. He was replaced by Sir Douglas Haig.

In spite of the debacle at Loos, the 46th Division made a name for itself there. At a crucial stage of the battle, it was considered that no progress could be made until certain German positions had been either captured or destroyed: these were known as the Hohenzollern Redoubt and Fosse 8. The redoubt was 'a large enclosed entrenchment wired all around',[13] and Fosse 8, nearby, was one of a number of fosses, the pit-heads of coal mines. Part of each pit-head was a wheel house ninety or a hundred feet high, which made an excellent observation post, though it attracted enemy fire. Both the Hohenzollern Redoubt and Fosse 8 had been captured at an earlier stage of the battle, and both had been lost again.

**The Hohenzollern Redoubt**
A scene during the attack of the 46$^{th}$ North Midland Division on 13$^{th}$ October, 1915
"The cloud of smoke and gas can be seen in the centre and left of this picture. Bursting shells in the center and the right. The British trenches and approaches can be traced by the chalk which has been excavated. Fosse 8 can just be made out behind the shrapnel bursting. The Hohenzollern Redoubt is this side of Fosse 8."
Photograph by courtesy of the Imperial War Museum.

The Division took its place in the front line during the night of 12th/13th October, with the task of retaking these two positions. Eddy reconnoitred the ground and decided to proceed 'as in siege warfare', by approaching his objectives trench by trench, and to attack as he did so with bombs.[14] He was overruled, however, and ordered to make what would be, in effect, one great rush.[15] To make matters worse, there was a shortage of bombs, and his men had been supplied with 'bags containing anything that looked like a bomb, old rifle grenades without sticks and old patterns without means of ignition.'[16] And, as if that was not bad enough, a preliminary gas attack simply eliminated the element of surprise from the operation.

The attack began on 13th October, in broad daylight; it was pressed hard, but no man's land and every part of the German lines were covered by machine gun posts and it was doomed. Some of the North Midlanders reached the Redoubt and others reached the group of miners' cottages at the pit-head, but those who were not killed or severely wounded were driven back or forced to withdraw for lack of grenades. Most of the casualties occurred in the first ten minutes, but the fighting went on throughout the night and into the next day, and the final figure for the Division's losses was 3,750.[17] Two Victoria Crosses were won;[18] and Eddy was mentioned in despatches,[19] which by this time meant only that he figured in a separate list of men considered worthy of special notice.

The devastating effect of the German machine guns at Loos is illustrated by one of the stories told by Robert Graves in *Goodbye to All That*.[20] A young officer had led his platoon over the top and, having met machine gun fire, had ordered the men to lie down. When he ordered them to get up again, none of them moved. He shouted at the them and called them cowards; whereupon his platoon-sergeant, who was wounded, gasped out 'Not cowards, sir. Willing enough. But they're all f---king dead'. It was at Loos, too, that Rudyard Kipling's son, John, was killed, and the blow to Kipling and his wife was all the greater for the fact that his body was never found.

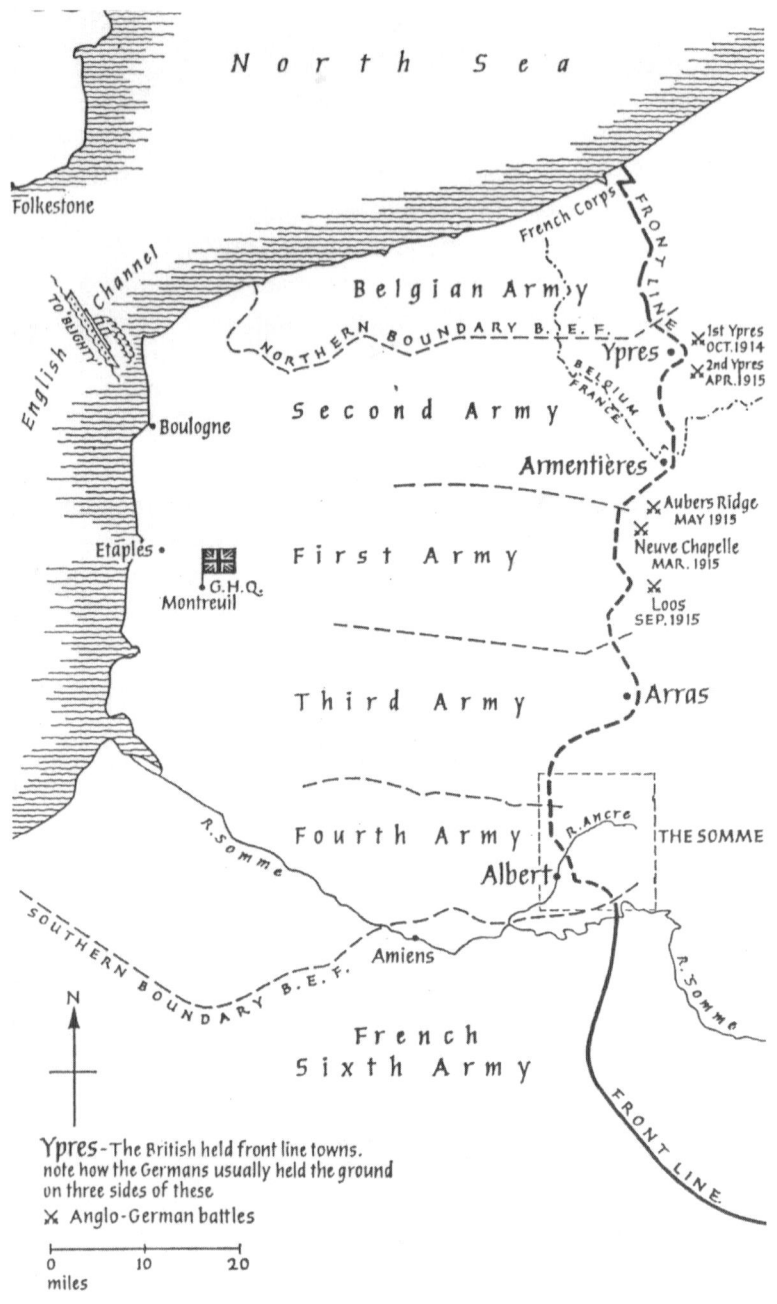

**The British Zone, June 1916**
From: *The First Day of The Somme*, by Martin Middlebrook

It was when Eddy had witnessed the destruction of his Division, at Loos on 13$^{th}$ October, that he decided to stop writing his regular letters to the King, for fear of showing his true feelings.[21] As it happened, the King visited France soon afterwards: he inspected representatives of units of XI Corps, of which the 46$^{th}$ Division was one, on 28$^{th}$ October; and he took the opportunity of thanking Eddy for his letters, in the hearing of others. 'The next day', Eddy recorded in a private memo, 'General Haking who commanded the XI Corps came to me and asked whether I was in the habit of writing to the King. I told him exactly what I had done. He then informed me that I had incurred the severe displeasure of a higher military authority, viz. Sir Douglas Haig, Commander of the 1$^{st}$ Army.'[22]

That day, 28$^{th}$ October, was one that would not be forgotten by the King or his staff. Later in the day, when he was inspecting units of the Royal Flying Corps, there was an accident: his horse, which was said to be accustomed to all the noises of war, was frightened by the men's cheers and threw him. 'The wretched animal reared up like a rocket and came over backwards,' wrote one of Sir John French's staff afterwards. 'No one had time to do anything. It looked as if H.M. must be badly injured.'[23] Fortunately, however, H.M. was not badly injured, but he returned to England on a hospital ship and was carried into Buckingham Palace on a stretcher.[24]

Towards the end of 1915, there appeared to be a need for a strategic reserve of troops to protect British interests in the East. It was decided that such a reserve should be assembled in Egypt, and that what was left of the 46$^{th}$ Division should be part of it. The Division began to embark at Marseilles on 1$^{st}$ January, 1916, but not all its units had reached Egypt, or sailed, before they were recalled to the Western Front. Two battalions, meanwhile, had been fortunate enough to spend some time in conditions of unaccustomed luxury at Marseilles, on board a requisitioned Cunard liner: 'There were stewards on board and officers all had comfortable cabins and the men bunks. Food was good, hot and plentiful.'[25]

**General Sir Douglas Haig**
Later Field Marshal The Earl Haig
Drawing in black chalk by Sir Muirhead Bone.
The artist was the first Official War Artist.
This drawing was made at the Front in 1916.
By courtesy of the Imperial War Museum.

At the end of 1915, too, the Allies, Britain, France, Russia and Italy, agreed to launch simultaneous offensives in their respective theatres in the following summer; Britain and France to act together on the Somme. The recall of the 46th Division was due to the need not only to prepare for the Somme but also, more urgently, to support the French, the Germans having launched a major offensive at Verdun on 21st February. A diversionary attack by the Germans at Givenchy, between Neuve Chapelle and Loos, at the same time, had driven the French off Vimy Ridge; it was in the new front line here, in place of the French, that the Division found itself in March and April.

The Division's task at Vimy Ridge was to hold the line: it was not a comfortable one. The Germans occupied the high ground above, and the trenches taken over from the French had not been well constructed or maintained, so that the North Midlanders had to look to their defences. They called one of their trenches Wortley Avenue.[26] Tunnelling and mining was a routine form of trench warfare on the Western Front, but the ground in the sector was particularly well suited to it; a state of affairs of which both sides were able to take advantage. There was both rain and snow during this time, and the men had often to stand for hours in mud or water. 'So much for Vimy,' wrote one regimental historian. 'From March 16th to April 23rd it cost the battalion 20 killed and 76 wounded, to say nothing of the number who went sick...'[27]

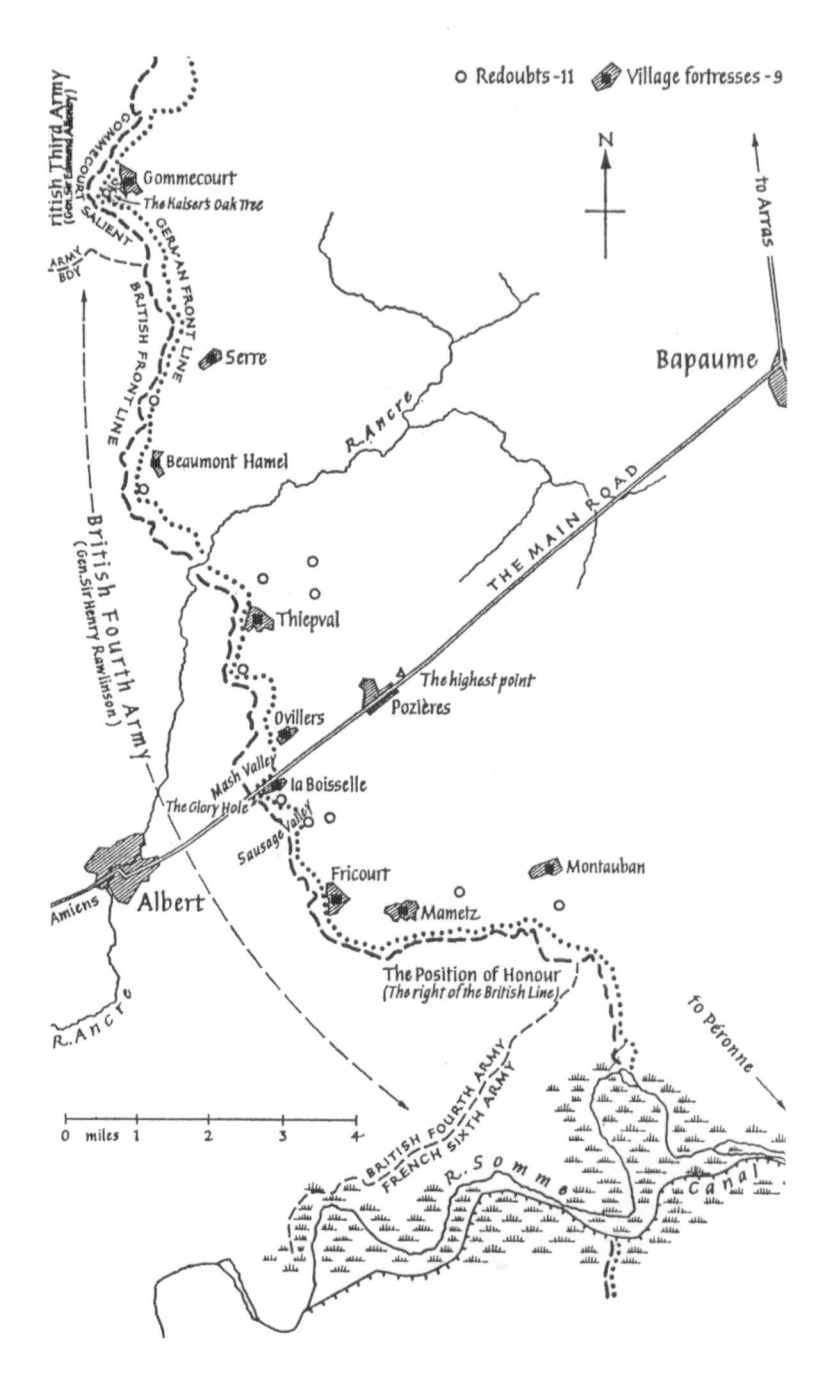

**The Somme Front, June 1916**
From: *The First Day of The Somme*, by Martin Middlebrook

# CHAPTER SIXTEEN

## THE GREAT WAR (2)
## THE FIRST DAY OF THE SOMME

THE FIRST DAY of the Somme was one of the saddest days of the Great War for Britain and her Allies. It had an added poignancy for Eddy, because it marked what was, to all intents and purposes, the end of his active military career.

The 46$^{th}$ Division had been withdrawn from Vimy for training for the part that it was expected to play in the Anglo-French offensive of the Somme, planned at the end of 1915. Already, at Vimy, its strength had been built up by fresh drafts of men from England. The plans that had been made for this Anglo-French offensive had had to be modified, however, as a consequence of an intensification of the German offensive at Verdun: the British Expeditionary Force's aims were now to be, first and foremost, to break through the German lines on the Somme; but also, secondly to relieve the French of German pressure at Verdun.

General Sir Douglas Haig, Commander-in-Chief of the British Expeditionary Force, gave General Sir Henry Rawlinson and his 4$^{th}$ Army the task of leading the attack. The 46$^{th}$ Division was part of the 3$^{rd}$ Army, under General Sir Edmund Allenby, and that was given a separate assignment: it was to create a diversion at Gommecourt, on the left; it was also to capture the Gommecourt salient. Allenby was not happy about this, chiefly because there was to be a gap one mile wide between the 4$^{th}$ Army and the 3$^{rd}$ Army, which would deprive the smaller 3$^{rd}$ of the support that it would otherwise have been given by the larger 4$^{th}$. He cannot have been happy, either, about the strength of his army: he had a single corps, made up of two territorial divisions, the 46$^{th}$ (North Midland) Division and the 56$^{th}$ (London) Division.

**Captain Reginald Young, Adjutant,
2nd Battalion The Middlesex Regiment,
winning the Military Cross in action in the trenches
during the Battle of the Somme, 1st July, 1916.**
By Stanley L. Wood
By courtesy of the Director, National Army Museum, London.

The detailed planning for the 3$^{rd}$ Army's assignment was left by Allenby to his Corps Commander, General Sir Thomas Snow. The lack of resources available to them ruled out a direct frontal attack, and Snow decided that the two divisions should work their way round the salient, the 46$^{th}$ from the right and the 56$^{th}$ from the left, until they met. He knew that his men would draw fire from three directions as they moved round the salient, but no other option presented itself. Significantly, in view of what followed, he pointed out to Eddy that the effectiveness of their diversion would be time-limited; reminded him that they would have no reserves; and instructed him to advance only when the German defences had been destroyed by British artillery.[1]

It was 1$^{st}$ July. The Gommecourt sector had had the worst of the weather during the night, and the men had been floundering about in water and mud; to make matters worse, heavy shelling had caused many casualties. A British artillery bombardment of the German lines began at 6.45, as it had begun every morning for a week, but this morning it ceased at 7.30 instead of 7.45. Then, all along the front line, signals were given and the men went over the top, to meet deadly fire. At Gommecourt, there was some confusion, as a British smoke screen hid British objectives, and the effects of a generous allocation of rum made themselves felt. As often as not, men who reached the German wire found it undamaged by the artillery bombardment.[2]

The 56$^{th}$ Division is said to have been the best of the territorial divisions in France at that time.[3] It fought its way round the salient, as planned, and at least one party arrived within sight of its rendezvous with the 46$^{th}$, only to find itself facing a strong force of the enemy. What was left of the 56$^{th}$ might have been recalled before it was too late, but it was not, and it was trapped. It might be said that the 46$^{th}$ Division had little of which to boast: only small parties of men reached the German trenches, and of these men most became either casualties or prisoners. 'July 1. "Z" Day failure,' reads the diary of one officer, the last word heavily underlined. 'All the old fellows gone and the Division's reputation lost.'[4]

Later in the day, Snow ordered the 46th Division to try again to link up with the 56th and cut off the salient. Eddy could not ignore this order, but neither could he ignore the opinion of his own officers that another attack would be hopeless. He must have reflected, too, that the order was at odds with what Snow had had to say to him before the action began. It was true that the salient was still in German hands, but a diversion had been created. In an impossible situation, he compromised and decided on a token attack by just two companies. What happened then was that orders were given but cancelled before they could be carried out, in all cases but one, by his officers on their own initiative. A single platoon attacked, in ignorance of the fact that its orders had been cancelled, and only one of its men returned.

The Battle of the Somme lasted four and a half months, in which time the British armies advanced no more than eight miles and suffered no less than 400,000 casualties.[5] On that first day of the battle, it was only the armies' right wing that gained ground, but since it moved north rather than east it could scarcely be said to have advanced. On that day alone there were more than 57,000 casualties.[6] 'The casualties suffered by the British on the opening day of the Somme stand comparison, not only with other battles, but with complete wars,' Martin Middlebrook has written. 'The British Army's loss on that one day easily exceeds its battle casualties in the Crimean War, the Boer War and the Korean War combined.'[7]

Martin Middlebrook has noted that senior officers of the 46th Division found it so hard to believe the figures for their losses, at the end of the day, that they sent out search and rescue parties for men they felt sure must be trapped.[8] In spite of these figures, however Middlebrook has pointed out, the 46th had fewer casualties than any other complete division; this, he has argued, shows that 'Maj.- Gen. Stuart Wortley had managed to save most of his division'.[9] Eddy was relieved of his command, and it was held by

**British troops in a support trench
awaiting their turn to advance 1ˢᵗ July, 1916.**
Note the wire cutters attached to the rifle.
Photograph by courtesy of the Imperial War Museum.

some that he had been penalised for losing too many of his men; in Middlebrook's view, the opposite is more likely to have been the case.[10]

On 2nd July, Snow wrote to Allenby, 'I regret to have to report that the 46th Division in yesterday's operation showed a lack of offensive spirit'.[11] He went on to say that he had attributed the Division's failings to its commander's age and constitution, and to recommend that Eddy should be moved to a training post; for which, Snow put in diplomatically, he was particularly well qualified. Allenby forwarded this report to Haig on 3rd July, and Haig, in turn, on 4th July, forwarded it to the War Office, which was still vacant following the death of Lord Kitchener. Haig emphatically endorsed Snow's recommendation that Eddy should be moved. 'I am not prepared to accept him as a Divisional Commander again in this country', he said.[12]

Eddy returned to England at once; it is needless to say that he was appalled by what had happened. He protested at the slur to the 46th Division and himself at the time, and he continued to protest. He was able to point out that Snow's report to Allenby was written before his own report to Snow on the events of the day could have been received, and also that Snow actually sent a message of congratulation to the 46th Division.[13] Later, he discovered that the message of congratulation was not among the relevant papers at the War Office, and he suggested that it had never been seen by Allenby or Haig.[14] Snow sent his congratulations to the Division after having received Eddy's report, but his censure of Eddy and the Division had already gone to Allenby.

No other general was relieved of his command as a result of the events of 1st July, though the part that Eddy had played in the shambles was a relatively small one. Ironically, too, the brutal fact is that his job had been to draw German fire; and he had succeeded in it. Perhaps Allenby and Snow believed that if the 3rd Army, and in particular the 46th Division, had achieved more, the 4th Army would have been able to achieve more, but military historians have

**The Territorials at Pozieres 1916**
By William Barns Wollen
By courtesy of the Director, National Army Museum, London.

not taken this view. Allenby and Snow could not divest themselves completely of responsibility for the 3$^{rd}$ Army's performance, and they may have been concerned for their own positions. 'One feels,' Martin Middlebrook has concluded, 'that Stuart Wortley was a scapegoat.'[15]

In what became for Eddy a campaign to clear his name, he referred to the matter of his letters to the King: it was, as he said, ' a side issue which had its importance'.[16] Eddy was asked by the King to write to him every week, and he made sure that the Commander-in-Chief, Sir John French, was aware of this. He was later informed, however, that 'a higher military authority' was displeased about it, the clear implication being this was Sir Douglas Haig. It may not have been coincidence that, at the time of the higher military's authority's displeasure, Haig was intriguing against French:[17] he may well have been worried about what Eddy had been saying to the King. Haig had succeeded French by the time Eddy was dismissed, but prejudice may have influenced the decision.

Not many of those involved in the affair showed any concern for Eddy, but Snow was one who did. As early as 5$^{th}$ July he wrote to one of Haig's staff to try to undo some of the damage that he could see he had done.[18] Referring to his report, he insisted that he had not intended it to be read as an indictment of Eddy's 'military character'; no one familiar with Eddy's career, he maintained, could interpret it as such. 'The fact is,' he went on, 'that at his age, he was as a Divisional Commander, in a position the duties of which he had not the physical strength to perform, 'It was meant well, but it must have been cold comfort to Eddy, who was shown the letter.

# CHAPTER SEVENTEEN

## IRELAND

GENERAL HAIG, in his letter to the War Office endorsing General Snow's comments on Eddy's part in the Gommecourt affair, having stated that he had relieved him of his command and would not have him back, recommended that he should be given 'employment at home in training troops, for which his long experience fits him'.[1] This might be thought to have been intended to damn him with faint praise, but it was true, even if it was not all that there was to be said about him: Eddy was an experienced trainer of troops, with a distinguished record as a fighting soldier. He was not an experienced commander of large formations of men in the field, but no army commander then could have claimed great experience in the sort of warfare being waged on the Western Front.

Writing to the War Office, from the Turf Club, in Piccadilly, Eddy reported his arrival in England from France on $6^{th}$ July, 1916.[2] He was without an appointment for nearly six months, but on $23^{rd}$ December he assumed command of the $65^{th}$ ($2^{nd}$ Lowland) Division. The $65^{th}$ Division was one of the reserve units of the Territorial Force that had a purely wartime existence: it was formed in Scotland between August 1914 and August 1915; in March 1916 it moved to England; and in January 1917 it moved to Ireland, and set up its divisional headquarters at the Curragh, in County Kildare. The anticlimax of Eddy's career had brought him back to the place in which it had begun, forty years before; his relations, the Droghedas, were long gone.

His new appointment gave him responsibility for the training of the $65^{th}$ Division; it also gave him a share in the responsibility that the army in Ireland had to act in support of the Civil Power, when called on to do so. Civil Power was vested in the Lord Lieutenant, though it was wielded in practice by the Chief Secretary. The main protagonists in the problematic situation of Ireland, however, were the leaders of the various political factions, Nationalist Home Rulers, Republican Sinn Feiners and Unionists, in Ireland, and the Prime Minister and the Leader of the Opposition in England. This situation was all the more problematical for the fact that differences lay not only between Ireland and England but also between the Liberal and the Conservative Parties in England.

The year that Eddy spent in Ireland, 1917, happened to be one of relative calm, but that could not have been predicted: time was running out for the English in Ireland, but some did not believe it, and those who did could not agree on what should be done about it. Gladstone had begun the process of handing over Irish affairs to the Irish people between 1868 and 1871, with the disestablishment of the church and the reform of land laws, but his Home Rule Bills of 1886 and 1893 had been rejected by the House of Commons and the House of Lords, respectively. The power of the Lords to block bills passed by the Commons was curtailed by the Parliament Act of 1911, and Asquith's Home Rule Bill of 1912, having passed the Commons, had to be allowed to pass the Lords in 1914.

The Bill duly became the Act, but the outbreak of war in 1914 led to the postponement of its implementation; this, in turn, produced a dangerous atmosphere of suspense and uncertainty in Ireland. To make matters worse, the future of Ulster had not been settled by the Bill, chiefly because there was no discernible means of settling it. Irish Nationalist votes had been necessary to pass the Bill, and they were still required to keep the Liberal Government in power. Northern Irish Unionists, supported by members of the Conservative Party, however, were prepared to fight to escape Home Rule since it meant rule from Dublin. Various compromises were considered, but none could be found that was any more acceptable to all parties than the Bill as it was.

Even before the outbreak of war complicated the situation, ominous signs of tension were there for all to see. Militant groups of Irishmen, north and south, were arming themselves, sometimes openly; but even more serious than this was the so-called Curragh Incident of March 1914, sometimes misnamed the Curragh Mutiny. Rumour had it that pre-emptive military action was to be taken against extreme Unionists in Ulster, but there were many officers at the Curragh, from which base such action would be likely to be launched, whose sympathies lay with the Unionists, and between fifty and sixty of them, including General Hubert Gough, announced themselves ready to resign their commissions rather than take part.

Gough crossed to London to find some way out of this predicament for himself and his officers, and enlisted the aid of the Director of Military Operations at the War Office, General Henry Wilson. Together, they succeeded in extracting from the Minister for War, Colonel John Seely, an assurance that military action would not be taken in Ulster; but Seely had not had the Cabinet's authority to give that assurance, and he was forced to resign. Asquith then took temporary charge of Seely's department and repudiated his pledge. 'This indeed he was bound to do,' an Irish historian has written, 'but, although the incident went no further than this, it revealed, as by a vivid flash of lightning, that in this delicate area the loyalty of the army could no longer be taken for granted.'[3]

When war came, the Nationalist leader, John Redmond, and the Unionist leader, Edward Carson, encouraged their followers to join the British Army, and many of them did so. The most militant Irish nationalists did not join the British Army, of course: they made the most of the advantage that Britain's embattled state had given them. A revolutionary group, working under the aegis of a clandestine organisation called the Irish Republican Brotherhood, planned an insurrection and looked to Germany for support, but it was a hopeless venture: there was insufficient unity of purpose among those most closely involved; and there was little support in Ireland or Germany. Some of the group's leaders, however, believed that a blood sacrifice was worth making.

The uprising began in Dublin on Easter Monday, 24th April 1916. About 250 men, from organisations linked to the Brotherhood, led by Patrick Pearse, occupied the General Post Office, which was their headquarters, a number of other buildings across the city and St. Stephen's Green. The first shot was fired at the Castle, where a policeman was killed, but the attack was half-hearted and it brought police and troops to the scene in force. Pearse, at the Post Office, had no reliable means of coordinating or controlling the efforts of his men at their various strongpoints; they were heavily outnumbered and outgunned, and when artillery was used against them they could hold out no longer. What became known as the Easter Rising lasted six days.

The immediate effect of the emergency was that the whole of Ireland was placed under martial law, administered with a heavy hand by General Sir John Maxwell. Severity was to have been expected from Maxwell after what was, from the British point of view, an act of gross treachery, which caused hundreds of deaths and widespread destruction in Dublin and might have altered the course of the war; but the scope of the arrests, the secrecy of the courts martial and the mercilessness of the executions that took place under him were, in the end, more than either the Irish or the British people could stomach. Many of those arrested were interned in England, and though most were soon released their experiences did not redound to Britain's credit.

Martial law was not in force while Eddy was in Ireland, and no significant military action became necessary; the presence of troops, however, contributed to the keeping of the peace. That year saw the rise of Sinn Fein, at the expense of constitutional nationalism. Lloyd George, who had replaced Asquith as Prime Minister in December 1916, was too concerned with the progress of the war to give attention to Ireland, and her affairs were left to the Dublin authorities. A policy of arresting or re-arresting suspected trouble-makers became part of a vicious circle of action and reaction, which was held in check only with difficulty. It has been said that the regime was 'propped up by the military and increasingly dependent on them'.[4]

The 65th Division was disbanded in stages between December 1917 and March 1918, and Eddy was not given another appointment. A copy of a sympathetic letter to him from the former General Sir John French, now Field Marshal Lord French, dated 9th March, 1918, shows that he had hoped for another appointment in Ireland and been disappointed. French was writing as Commander-in-Chief Home Forces, but he was about to become Lord Lieutenant of Ireland.

> I'm truly sorry to tell you that it is impossible to keep you on in Ireland now that the 65th Division is broken up, and I can only thank you once again – at the conclusion of the long time of our service together – for all the help you have been and the energy you have shown.[5]

There is irony in the last phrase of this letter: Eddy was relieved of his command on the Somme because he had not shown enough energy.

But it is unlikely that he would have been happy in Ireland in the years that followed. Sinn Fein made great gains in the General Election of December 1918, and instead of claiming their seats at Westminster set up an Irish assembly in Dublin and issued a declaration of independence. This was tantamount to a declaration of war, and fighting broke out in many parts of the country. Atrocities were committed on both sides, but the Black and Tans conducted a continuous campaign of terror. At least one senior British officer refused to serve with these men.[6] It was only in 1921 that Lloyd George reached an agreement with moderate leaders of Sinn Fein, and one chapter of Irish history came to an end: the Irish Free State came into being as a self-governing dominion within the British Commonwealth.

# CHAPTER EIGHTEEN

## THE FAMILY IN WARTIME

IN THE WORDS of one writer, the Stuart Wortley family, at home at Highcliffe Castle in June 1914, 'saw the first movement of the curtain as it began to rise on one of the world's greatest human tragedies.'[1] Violet told the story.

> We were entertaining a party at Highcliffe for Whitsuntide, including Count and Countess Dubski; the Count was First Secretary at the Austrian Embassy. In the middle of dinner on Sunday night a telegram was handed to him. Heaving read it, he passed it across the table to his wife, and turning to me, in a voice which shook somewhat with emotion he announced the news of the assassination of the Archduke Ferdinand and his wife at Sarajevo.[2]

The significance of the assassination was by no means generally clear at the time, however. Violet later recorded having been shocked by the news, but disappointed that a ball at the Austrian Embassy would have to be cancelled.

Indeed, so unaware were the Stuart Wortleys of the imminence of war in Europe that Violet went ahead with a planned visit to France in July, taking with her their younger daughter, Bettine, who was then eighteen. When disquieting rumours were heard, she and her hostess went into Paris for news; they had lunch with the Austrian Ambassador, but he gave nothing away. At a couturier's establishment the same day she met a certain princess with German connections, who confided in her that, on account of those German connections, she was wanted by the police and was about to leave for Munich. Still not seriously worried, Violet decided that she and

130

Bettine ought to return to England; judging from her account of this episode, they returned on 1$^{st}$ August, three days before war began.

From the first, Eddy was intent on bringing the North Midland Division to the highest pitch of readiness as soon as possible; he cannot have had time to spare for Violet, and no doubt she understood that. No doubt, too, she followed his movements and the news from the front as closely as she could, but she had little to say about his war service when she came to write her books, and nothing at all about his fall from grace or his service in Ireland. She dated the start of some of her own war work from his Division's departure for France, and she mentioned the fact that, since her war work kept her in the capital, she bought a house in London, to which Eddy and their son, Rothesay, came occasionally on leave.

Rothesay had been at Eton and had gone on to Oxford; now twenty-two, he had been working in New York for some time, but had come home to train with the Hants Yeomanry and had joined the regular army. He was briefly on Eddy's Staff and equally briefly a Staff Captain with an infantry brigade, but his true metier was the Royal Flying Corps. He flew with fighter squadrons, one of which he eventually commanded, over the Western Front, and made a name for himself for his bravery and dash; he was awarded the MC in 1918.[3] Violet claimed to have witnessed one of his exploits, in the skies over London, during a period of training.

> In Belgrave Square one afternoon, suddenly I saw every pedestrian stop and look at the sky, and I looked, too. Just overhead was a Zeppelin! And not so very far behind a British fighter! It was only after the battle, and when my son that evening told me, that I knew it was Rothesay who was in pursuit of the raider. He might have shot it down had his Lewis gun not jammed.[4]

Violet worked with the YMCA, at first at Aldershot but afterwards in London. Her role at Aldershot was a humble one, but all she wrote about it was that it included the serving of the tea in the middle of the night on Farnborough station, from which troops departed for the front. 'The pitch-black platforms, the clustering groups of young soldiers, the silence observed,' she wrote, 'induced a sense of impending tragedy and depression.'[5] In London, however, she became involved in the organisation of women's part in the activities of the YMCA, with its National Secretary, Sir Arthur Yapp, and Princess Helena Victoria, Queen Victoria's granddaughter, one of its patrons. Not an overtly religious woman, she was impressed by what she called its 'mixture of religion and common-sense realism.'[6]

Violet could be down-to-earth in her approach to practical problems. Yapp and his colleagues were interested in the welfare of the large numbers of young servicemen loose on the streets of London at night. They realised that many of these young men were well able to look after themselves, but they were worried about those who might be too easily beguiled into parting with their money and their innocence. Representations to the proper authorities fell on deaf ears; and, while fresh moves were being considered, Violet and two of her friends decided to do what they could themselves. 'We would patrol the streets in the worst areas after midnight,' she wrote, 'and endeavour to shepherd half-drunken boys to safe lodgings...'[7]

Social life went on, but for Violet at least it was not possible ever to forget the war. Diversion and duty overlapped for her at the home of Jean Hamilton, wife of General Sir Ian Hamilton, who commanded the Allied land forces in the Dardanelles Campaign of 1915. Here, at tea-parties, she would support Lady Hamilton as she tried to keep up the spirits of the wives of officers serving with Sir Ian; it was no easy task, and in the end there were failure and losses to be faced. At Highcliffe, the war gave her a new neighbour; this was Sir Edward Goschen, who had been Ambassador at Berlin until the last moment of peace. He was 'a delightful companion, gently sarcastic, amusingly observant, above all as susceptible as a young man to youth and beauty'.[8]

There was not much entertaining at Highcliffe Castle during the war, but there is one particularly interesting entry in the Visitors' Book: this is the name Fred Milner, against the date 26$^{th}$ July, 1916.[9] Milner, as Sir Alfred Milner had been High Commissioner for South Africa before, during and after the Boer War; he was now Lord Milner, high in the counsels of government ministers; and he was soon to become a member of Lloyd George's small War Cabinet. His connection with the Stuart Wortleys is not clear, but his visit to Highcliffe took place only three weeks after Eddy's sad return to England from France, and it seems likely that there was some connection between the two events. Perhaps Milner was a go-between, a suggestion that, it must be admitted, leaves us little the wiser.

The Stuart Wortleys' elder daughter, Louise, was twenty-one in 1914; she and Bettine, their younger daughter, both worked in hospitals during the war: 'a grim enough initiation into adult life for two young girls whose outlook had been so sheltered', Violet remarked.[10] But their initiation was not grim in every respect: according to Violet, herself, there was 'a little hectic entertaining, impromptu dancing parties, and lunching out in restaurants';[11] and it may have been at some such occasion that Bettine met her first husband. This was Captain Allastair Edward Grant, of the 9$^{th}$ Lancers, who appears in the Visitor's Book as Eddie Grant. They were married in 1917 but divorced five years later.[12]

# CHAPTER NINETEEN

## RETIREMENT (1)

RETIREMENT BEGAN for Eddy, in effect, when his appointment in Ireland came to an end, in March 1918. It cannot have been easy for him to accept the fact that his career had come to an end at the same time, since the war was not over; indeed, in that month of March 1918 a German offensive on the Western Front put victory in the balance again; and he had unfinished business. His campaign to clear his name continued, and it is doubtful if he ever fully came to terms with what had happened to him. In May 1920 he wrote to Winston Churchill, who had become Minister for War in Lloyd George's new administration, to plead his cause, and though his letter has been lost a signed draft of Churchill's reply is part of the record.[1]

It was not an unfriendly reply, but neither was it un-businesslike. 'My dear Stuart Wortley,' Churchill began, 'I have read your letter of May 4$^{th}$, but I am not clear in my mind as to what you really want; you do not make any specific request.' Eddy had evidently maintained that General Snow's report of 2$^{nd}$ July 1917, was not to be read as critical of him as a soldier: Snow himself, Churchill pointed out, had implied as much in the same report; it was Eddy's age, and the lack of vigour that went with age, to which his Corps Commander had drawn attention. Eddy then claimed that Lord French had recommended him for a knighthood; what Churchill had to say about this was that he had had the relevant records examined, and that no such recommendation had been found.

Unfortunately, his family could not be a comfort to him at first. In November 1919, Rothesay married Marie Louise Edwardes, a celebrated Canadian prima donna, known professionally as Edvina or Madam Edvina. She has been described as a 'highly sophisticated woman of great integrity, warmth and charm',[2] but she was not the wife that Eddy or Violet would have chosen for him;[3] apart from any other consideration, she was forty-one and he was twenty-seven. She had been widowed twice, and she had two daughters. But disappointment paled into insignificance beside the sadness that followed. Rothesay developed diabetes mellitus, and though insulin was discovered at about this time it came into clinical use too late to save him; there was a remission and then a relapse, and he died in December 1926.

Bettine's first marriage failed almost at once, and it ended in divorce in 1922. Five years later, however, she was happily married to Montagu Bertie, Earl of Abingdon and Lindsey. Meanwhile, in 1924, to the satisfaction of Eddy and Violet, Louise married Sir Percy Loraine, Bart, then British Minister at Tehran. They had met in the years before the war, in Italy; he had been on Sir Rennell Rodd's staff at the Embassy at Rome. Neither of them was young: she was thirty-one and he was forty-four; but Rodd, who knew her well, is quoted as having said that he was the first man of whom she had ever been particularly fond.[4] She was described at the time as 'a very handsome woman of thirty, she was tall and dark, with fine eyes...'[5]

In 1923 there was a family reunion at Highcliffe. Eddy's brother Ralph, the third of the brothers, who lived in America, was visiting England, and there came to meet him at the Castle: Major General Sir Richard Stuart Wortley, the fourth of the brothers; Sir Richard's wife, Maud; Sir Richard's son and daughter, Jim and Marjorie; Lord Carlton, otherwise Archibald Montagu-Stuart-Wortley-Mackenzie, eldest son of the first of the brothers, Frank, 2nd Earl of Wharncliffe; Elfreda, Lady Carlton; Lady Rachel Sturgis, Frank's daughter; and Sir Mark Sturgis, Rachel's husband.[6] They were not to know it then, but the earldom of Wharncliffe was to pass, in due course, to Ralph's American grandson.

Ralph had left England while still in his teens, and it was either at this reunion or on an earlier visit that Violet decided to show him something of his native land. The chronology that she followed in her writing leaves the year uncertain. There was staying at Highcliffe at the time, whenever this was, a young Canadian called Jim Dunn, who had a car that was described by Violet as being as super-charged as he was himself. In this car, Dunn whirled Ralph and others round the countryside, one day concentrating on the cathedrals of southern England; Violet recorded the occasion.

> We achieved four cathedrals in one day. Beginning with Winchester, we next gave Salisbury a brief but intensive look-over, included Glastonbury and Wells in our programme and finally drew up breathlessly at Exeter.[7]

After that, Ralph said he never wished to see another cathedral.

There is a discrepancy between the Castle Visitors' Book and Violet's autobiography in the dates given for a visit by the Duke and Duchess of Aosta: the Visitors' Book gives 1923 and the autobiography 1928. Violet had met the previous Duke of Aosta, a nephew of the King Umberto of Italy, and his family, while staying with the Rodds, when the present Duke had been a boy. This Duke had recently married a daughter of the Pretender of the time to the throne of France, and they brought with them to Highcliffe her brother, known then as Prince Henry of France. When his father died, Prince Henry 'succeeded' as Pretender, and was thereafter known as the Comte de Paris. He was seventeen at the time of the visit; Violet remembered him turning somersaults on the lawn.

Eddy did not live to follow the fortunes of the Comte de Paris or the Duke of Aosta. The Comte hoped to revive the royalist cause in France, but was disappointed almost at once. An opinion poll held in 1945 showed that 'only 6 per cent of the nation thought that a royalist party had an important role in France and about 75 per cent thought not;'[8] the situation has not changed significantly since. The Duke became Viceroy of Abyssinia when that country was annexed by Italy in 1936. He was the representative of King Victor Emmanuel; and, caught up though he was in Mussolini's

**Queen Mary at Highcliffe Castle
with Edward and Violet Stuart Wortley**
From: *Highcliffe Castle*, by Tahu Hole

adventures, he deplored the Duce's policies. He did his best to prevent war between Italy and England in 1940; then he did what he saw to be his duty as Viceroy, until the Italian army in Abyssinia was forced to surrender in 1941.

The most distinguished of the visitors to the Castle in those days was Queen Mary, who was staying with the Earl and Countess of Shaftsbury, at Wimborne St. Giles, at the time. She was interested in antiques, and she was not disappointed with what she was shown. Little had changed in the house since Lord Stuart de Rothesay built it and furnished it, between 1830 and 1835, after his years as Ambassador at Paris. Lord Stuart was not a collector as was, for instance, his friend Lord Yarmouth, later Marquess of Hertford, but he was a discriminating purchaser: there was furniture from the Empire period and the Restoration, some of which had belonged to Marshal Ney; there were prints, drawings and paintings; there were ceramics, and there was sculpture. Much of all this now forms the Bettine, Lady Abingdon Collection at the Victoria and Albert Museum.

There are many entries for members of the family in the Visitors' Book, particularly for Bettine in the years between 1922 and 1927, but Nellie Melba has the most entries for a friend. In the context of a reminiscence of Melba, Violet once remarked that Eddy loved music; though the prima donna was not always ready to sing for friends on private occasions, she added, Eddy could usually persuade her.

> ESW was passionately fond of music, and to please him she would succumb to persuasion and sitting down to the piano and would sing, playing her own accompaniment, the simple melodies that she herself loved.[9]

It may have been Eddy who persuaded her to sing for the congregation one Sunday evening in Highcliffe parish church; she chose Gounod's *Ave Maria*.

The church was part of Eddy's life at Highcliffe. He treated his position as Patron of the Living as a privilege and a duty: he had nominated the Reverend Frederick Gray in 1908; in 1919, when Gray resigned, he put forward the Reverend Frederick Evans; in 1925 Evans moved on and he chose the Reverend Charles Gould to follow him. He was a long-standing member of the Parochial Church Council, and he sat on other church committees from time to time. He was a generous contributor to church funds, and to funds that were more specifically charitable. Unless he was away, he was usually to be seen in church, at least once on Sunday, occupying the front pew on the right. The Castle family had its own door into the church: it is still there, between the south transept and the cloister.

He had the golf course at Highcliffe laid out on his own land in 1913, and later had it extended. He supported the cricket club, from the driver's seat of his car in the last years of his life. He took an interest in the Working Men's Club, where his portrait by Archibald Stuart Wortley now hangs. Appropriately, he became President of the Highcliffe Branch of the British Legion. Between 1911 and 1922 there was a Scout Troop at Highcliffe called General Stuart Wortley's Own: he must have sympathised with the aims of the founder of the Scout movement, General Sir Robert Baden-Powell, later Lord Baden-Powell, whose experiences in South Africa he had come close to sharing; but they did not know each other.

Sometimes, Eddy and Violet would allow the Castle grounds to be used for a parish or village event, such as a fête or a garden party. Occasionally, too, they would open the Castle itself. They made an admission charge, and though this was, no doubt, always in support of some good cause it amused one visitor to see 'the General' holding out his hand at the door. Eddy is often said to have been quiet and reserved in his manner, at least at home and at that time of his life: this visitor, however, a boy at the time, had the distinct impression that there was amusement and even mischief behind the unpromising front.[10]

# CHAPTER TWENTY

## RETIREMENT (2)

THERE WERE VISITS to the houses of friends and neighbours in Hampshire, part of which county Christchurch, including Highcliffe, still was. Some of these houses and their owners had links with Highcliffe and the Stuarts, in history or legend: Somerley, the home of the Earls of Normanton, was said to be the house from which Lord Stuart de Rothesay disappeared one evening during a ball, to reappear in Iceland (sic) a few days later without explanation of his behaviour, except that 'paying visits bored him;'[1] Hurn Court was then the home of the Earl of Malmesbury, descendant of that distinguished diplomat the first bearer of the title, who memorably described Lord Stuart de Rothesay as 'the Duke of Wellington's right hand man in the Peninsular War'.[2]

By this time, Palace House, Beaulieu, and the 10,000 acres that went with it, belonged to Eddy's cousin, John Scott Montagu, who had succeeded his father as 2$^{nd}$ Lord Montagu of Beaulieu. He was a many-sided man, whose greatest achievement was to make the use of the car a part of everyday life, by his patronage and by his written and spoken advocacy. It was as a sportsman, however, that Eddy knew him best. The 10,000 acres, surrounded by forest, river and sea, provided good shooting and fishing; there was hunting in the New Forest, but the 2$^{nd}$ Lord Montagu had given up this form of sport in his youth: 'with him', his biographers wrote, 'a horse was apt to be looked upon as an animal of which speed was required rather than pleasure'.[3]

There were visits to country houses in other parts of England, too. Violet mentioned Chatsworth, Kedleston, Knole, Nostell, Waddesdon and Welbeck, among others; of these, in her view, Welbeck was the most sumptuous but Waddesdon the most luxurious. She mentioned portraits that caught her eye in some of

**Violet Stuart Wortley**
By Simon Elwes R.A.
The artist married Violet's niece Grace Rodd. He painted this portrait with his left hand in or about 1953, when he had taught himself to work with his left hand, his right arm having been affected by a stroke in 1944.

these houses, but she did not mention one that must have been brought to Eddy's attention at Waddesdon: this is George Romney's portrait of Lord Stuart de Rothesay's mother, Lady Stuart, which was sold to Baron Ferdinand de Rothschild by Lady Waterford in 1890, or thereabouts.[4] Cardiff Castle, restored by the 3rd Marquess of Bute, father of the Lord Bute of the time, without thought of expense, appears in Violet's list of rankings as the oldest house in which she and Eddy stayed.

London Society had recovered its pre-war vitality by 1924, according to Violet; but she hinted at disapproval of the fact that there had been an increase in the number of American hostesses. Perhaps for this reason, she made much of a dinner of the Gaelic Society in London, presided over by Lord Bute and attended by the Prince of Wales, later King Edward VIII, in full Highland dress. The members of the society, she said, were meeting 'to keep fresh and warm the sense of common ancestry, and a shared tradition'.[5] Among the Americans in London was Gordon Selfridge, to whom Highcliffe Castle was let whether or not Violet approved of him. Ironically, he claimed Scottish ancestry.[6]

Selfridge had come to England as a successful businessman in 1906, and three years later opened the department store in Oxford Street at which Londoners then wondered. It was between the years 1916 and 1925, intermittently though sometimes for long periods, that he rented or leased the Castle as a weekend retreat for himself and his family. He was fond of the place: it has been said that it represented stability in his life.[7] 'Alone', wrote his biographer, 'Selfridge was happiest in retiring to the brass-grilled library of Highcliffe, where he divided his time between reading and day-dreaming.'[8] He died a naturalised Englishman, and he chose to be buried in the churchyard at Highcliffe, where his mother and his wife already lay.

During the years in which the Castle was occupied by Selfridge or another of their tenants, Eddy and Violet made a home for themselves elsewhere in Highcliffe. When the war was over, Violet travelled abroad, often to the capitals at which her brother-in-law Sir Rennell Rodd, and son-in-law Sir Percy Loraine, were stationed as diplomats, where she could rely on being looked after and entertained. Judging from her writings, Eddy did not accompany her on her earlier travels; in 1929, however, they returned together to Egypt and the Sudan, where Loraine had recently been appointed High Commissioner, and later, following another visit to Egypt and the Sudan, there were visits to Cyprus, Ceylon, Burma, Bulgaria, Brazil, the Argentine and Chile.

On one of these trips to Egypt and the Sudan, the Governor-General of the Sudan, Sir John Maffey, invited Eddy to visit Omdurman on the anniversary of the great battle, and to address the troops there. This Eddy did, and his talk, as reported by Violet, is one of the few scraps of autobiography that we have.[9] In Cyprus, in holiday mode, they talked of settling on the island and growing oranges. In Brazil, they retraced the footsteps of Lord Stuart de Rothesay, when Sir Charles Stuart, who negotiated the treaty by which that country obtained its independence of Portugal in 1825. In Chile, in 1933, Eddy made his first flight in an aeroplane, which took Violet and him over the Andes, an episode from his later life that was picked out for mention in his obituary in *The Times*.[10]

It was in that year, 1933, that Eddy's health began to fail. When winter came he was advised to go abroad, and sometime after Christmas he and Violet travelled first to Portugal and then to Morocco. The climate did not help him as they had hoped it would; his condition deteriorated and he died on 18th March, 1934, at Tangier. There was a Memorial Service at Tangier, but the funeral took place at St. Mark's Church, Highcliffe. A bearer party from the King's Royal Rifles assisted at the burial in the churchyard, and a bugler sounded the Last Post and the Reveille.[11]

Obituarists were kind to him; the end of his career was glossed over. *The Times* called him 'a typical representative of the Regular Army of the late Victorian period', and implied, perhaps with greater truth than it knew, that adaptation to change had been difficult for him.

> A scion of an ancient family, famous for its wealth, influence, sporting tastes, and social activities, he was everywhere, from the Court downwards, universally popular. But after the South African War the conditions of his profession proved no longer congenial to one who had been brought up in other conditions. The ambitions and earlier promise of 'Eddie' (sic), as he was always known to numerous friends, consequently never came to full maturity.[12]

# BIBLIOGRAPHY

## UNPUBLISHED SOURCES AND ABBREVIATIONS

| | |
|---|---|
| Bod. Lib | Bodleian Library, Oxford. |
| Brit. Lib | British Library, London. |
| Fynemore | Mr Fynemore's Scrapbook: Sandgate and Shorncliffe, Vol. 2, 942.23 SAND. Folkestone Library |
| HRO | Hampshire Record Office, Winchester |
| LHCMA | Liddell Hart Centre for Military Archives, King's College, London (Lyttelton 1.) |
| PRO | Public Record Office, Kew |
| RGJMA: | Royal Green Jackets Museum Archives. |
| SA: WhM418 | Sheffield Archives: Wharncliffe Muniments. |
| SAD | Sudan Archive, Durham University. Wingate Papers. |
| Visitors' Book | Highcliffe Castle Visitors' Book: National Art Library, Victoria and Albert Museum, L3363 – 1990. |

## PUBLISHED SOURCES

Amery, L.S. (Ed.)
    The Times History of the War in South Africa 1899-1902. Sampson Low, Marston, London, 7 vols, 1900-1909.

Beresford, Admiral Lord Charles.
    Memoirs. Methuen, London, 2 vols, 1914.

Bond, Brian, and Cave, Nigel. (Ed.)
    Haig: A Reappraisal 70 Years On. Leo Cooper, Barnsley, 1999.

Burke's Peerage and Baronetage.

Bülow, Prince von
    Memoirs, Putnam, London, 3 vols, 1931.

Cannon, John. (Ed.)
    The Oxford Companion to British History. Oxford, 1997.

Cecil, Lamar.
    Wilhelm II. University of North Carolina, 2 vols, 1996.

Charteris, John.
> At GHQ. Cassell, London, 1931.

Churchill (1), Winston S.
> The River War. Prion, London, 1997.

Churchill (2), Winston S.
> London to Ladysmith via Pretoria. Longmans Green, London, 1900.

Colvile, H.E.
> History of the Sudan Campaign. H.M. Stationery Office, London, 3 vols, 1889.

Cowles, Virginia.
> The Kaiser. Collins, London, 1963.

Craig, F.W.S. (Ed.)
> British Parliamentary Results 1885-1918. Parliamentary Research Services, Dartmouth, 1974.

Craig, Gordon A.
> Germany 1866-1945. Oxford, 1978.

Cromer, The Earl of.
> Modern Egypt. Macmillan, London, 2 vols, 1908.

Dictionary of National Biography.

Edmonds, Sir James E. (Ed.)
> History of the Great War: Military Operations in France and Belgium 1915. Macmillan, London, vol.4, 1928.

Ensor, Sir Robert.
> England 1870-1914. Oxford, 1936.

Fielding, Daphne.
> The Duchess of Jermyn Street. Eyre and Spottiswoode, London, 1964.

Fitzgerald, Penelope.
> Edward Burne-Jones. Michael Joseph, London, 1975.

Franklin, Robert.
> Lord Stuart de Rothesay. Images, Upton-upon-Severn, 1993.

Gilbert, Martin.
> First World War. HarperCollins, London, 1995.

Gladwyn, Cynthia.
>The Paris Embassy. Collins, London, 1976.

Gooch, G.P. and Temperley, Harold. (Ed.)
>British Documents on the Origins of the War 1898-1914.
>>H.M. Stationery Office, London, vol.6. 1930.

Gove, Michael.
>Religion turns into history. In *The Times* 12$^{th}$ September, 2001.

Graves, Robert.
>Goodbye to All That. Penguin Books, London, 1960.

Hansard: The Parliamentary Debates (4$^{th}$ Series).

Hare, Augustus J.C.
>The Story of Two Noble Lives. George Allen, London, 3 Vols,
>>1893

Hart, B.H. Liddell.
>Memoirs. Cassell, London, 2 vols, 1965.

Hole, Tahu.
>Highcliffe Castle. Printed privately, 1972.

Howard, Christopher H.D. (Ed.)
>The Diary of Edward Goschen 1900-1914.
>>Royal Historical Society, London, 1980.

Kochanski, Halik.
>Sir Garnet Wolseley; Victorian Hero. The Hambledon Press,
>>London, 1999.

*King's Royal Rifle Corps Chronicle, The.*

*London Gazette, The*

Lee, Sir Sidney.
>King Edward VII. Macmillan, London, 2 vols, 1927.

MacGregor, Sir Charles. (Ed.)
>The Second Afghan War 1878-1880. John Murray, London, 1908.

McPherson, James B.
>Edvina. The Encyclopaedia of Music of Canada.
>>University of Toronto, 1992.

Magnus, Phillip.
>King Edward the Seventh. John Murray, London, 1964.

Malmesbury, The Earl of.
    Memoirs of an Ex-Minister. Longmans, 2 vols, London, 1884.

Middlebrook, Martin.
    The First Day of the Somme: $1^{st}$ July, 1916. Penguin Books, London, 1984.

Milne, John.
    Footprints of the 1/ $4^{th}$ Leicestershire Regiment August 1914 – November 1918. Edgar Backus, Leicester, 1935.

*Morning Post, The.*

Pakenham, Thomas.
    The Boer War. Weidenfeld and Nicholson, London, 1979.

Palmer, Alan.
    The Kaiser: Warlord of the Second Reich, Phoenix, London, 1997.

Parliamentary Debates: see Hansard.

Pollock, John.
    Kitchener: the Road to Omdurman. Constable, London, 1998.

Pound, Reginald.
    Selfridge. Heinemann, London, 1960.

Robson, Brian (Ed.)
    Roberts in India. The Military Papers of Field Marshal Lord Roberts 1876 –1893. Alan Sutton for the Army Records Society, London, 1993.

Rodd, Sir (James) Rennell.
    Social and Diplomatic Memories, Second Series, 1894-1901. Edward Arnold, London, 1923.

St Aubyn, Giles.
    Edward VII. Collins, London, 1979.

Schweizer, Karl W. (Ed.)
    Lord Bute: Essays in Re-interpretation. Leicester University, 1988.

Shadbolt, Sydney. H.
    The Afghan Campaign of 1878-1880. Sampson, Low, Marston, Skarle and Rivington, London, 1882.

Steevens, G.W.
>With Kitchener to Khartoum. William Blackwood, Edinburgh and London, 1898.

Stenton, Michael, and Lees, Stephen.
>Who's Who of British Members of Parliament. The Harvester Press, Sussex, vol.2, 1886-1918, 1978.

Stuart Wortley, Rothesay.
>Letters to a Flying Officer, Oxford 1928.

Stuart Wortley (1) Violet.
>Magic in the Distance. Hutchinson, London, 1948.

Stuart Wortley (4), Violet.
>Life without Theory. Hutchinson, London 1946.

Stuart Wortley (5) Violet.
>Grow Old Along With Me. Secker and Warburg, London, 1952.

*Times, The.*

Treveylan, G.M.
>British History in the Nineteenth Century and After 1782-1919. Longmans, London, 1937.

Treves, Frederick.
>The Tale of a Field Hospital. Cassell, London, 1900.

Troubridge, Lady, and Marshall, Archibald.
>John Lord Montagu of Beaulieu, Macmillan, London, 1930.

Tweedsmuir, Susan.
>The Lilac and the Rose. Duckworth, London, 1952.

*Vanity Fair*

Vaughan, W.E. (Ed.)
>A New History of Ireland. Vol.6, Ireland Under the Union 11 (1870-1921). Oxford, 1996.

Waterfield, Gordon.
>Professional Diplomat. John Murray, London, 1973.

Waterhouse, Ellis.
>Waddesdon Catalogue of Paintings. Office du Livre, 1967.

Who Was Who

William II, Ex-Kaiser.
    My Memoirs 1878-1918. Cassell, London, 1922.

Wingate, Sir Reginald, Bart.
    Wingate of the Sudan. John Murray, London, 1955.

Wolfe, Charles.
    The Burial of Sir John Moore at Corunna. Palgrave's Golden Treasury. Oxford, 1994.

Wolff, Sir Henry Drummond.
    Rambling Recollections. Macmillan, London, 2 vols, 1908.

Zeldin, Theodore.
    France 1848-1945. Oxford, 2 vols, 1973.

# REFERENCES

## CHAPTER ONE
**Background and Early Life**

1. Schweizer, p.270
2. SA: WhM418. Francis Stuart Wortley to Lord Wharncliffe, 29th August, 1885.
3. Birth Certificate of Edward James Stuart Wortley
4. Eton College Archives
5. SA: WhM418. Francis Stuart Wortley to Lord Wharncliffe, 14th February, 1878.
6. RGJMA: Ref.0387, Box 2/1. Eddy to his mother, 12th October, 1879.
7. Army Lists
8. *Vanity Fair*, 26th October, 1899.
9. Gove
10. Information from the Director of the National Army Museum

## CHAPTER TWO
**Afghanistan**

1. Army Lists
2. Stuart Wortley (4), p.26
3. Ibid.
4. Ibid.
5. RGJMA: Ref.0387, Box 2/1. Eddy to his mother, 18th September, 1879.
6. Ibid.
7. Robson, p.112
8. RGJMA: Ref.0387, Box 2/1. Eddy to his mother, 12th October, 1879.
9. Ibid.
10. Ibid.
11. Stuart Wortley (4), p.26
12. MacGregor, p291
13. RGJMA: Ref.0387, Box 2/1. Eddy to his mother, 26th October, 1879.

14. Shadbolt, p.137
15. RGJMA: Ref.0387, Box 2/1. Eddy to his mother, 26th October, 1879.
16. MacGregor, p.299
17. RGJMA: Ref.0387, Box 2/1. Eddy to his mother, 21st December, 1879.
18. Ibid. Eddy's account of the action of the 12th and 13th December, 1879.
19. MacGregor, p.299
20. RGJMA: Ref.0387, Box 2/1. Eddy to his mother, 21st December, 1879.
21. MacGregor, p.299
22. Ibid. p.300
23. Ibid
24. RGJMA: Ref.0387, Box 2/1. Eddy to his mother, 21st December, 1879.
25. Ibid. Eddy to his mother, 11th March, 1880.
26. Ibid. Eddy to his mother, 22nd April, 1880.
27. Ibid. Eddy to his mother, 22nd August, 1880.
28. Stuart Wortley (4), p.27
29. Ibid

## CHAPTER THREE
**Egypt and the Sudan (1)**

1. Stuart Wortley (4), p.28
2. SA: WhM418. Eddy to Lord Wharncliffe, 10th August 1886.
3. HRO: 21M82, PZ5. Highcliffe Parish Magazine, April 1892.
4. Ibid.
5. Army List, January 1918, pt.2, p.3072.
6. Kochanski, p.144
7. Ensor, p.80
8. Rodd, p.46
9. SA: WhM418. Eddy to Lord Wharncliffe, 12th June 1883.
10. Who Was Who 1929 - 1940.
11. Rodd, p.46
12. SA: WhM418. Sir Evelyn Wood to Lord Wharncliffe, 6th May 1883
13. SA: WhM418. Various letters
14. Stuart Wortley (4), p.28

15. Brit. Lib. Add.MSS.51300, ff.173-176. Eddy to Augusta Gordon, 11th December 1885.
16. Colvile, v.2. p.44
17. Ibid.
18. *The Morning Post*, 16th June 1884, p.3
19. SAD. 250/1/6. Eddy to Reginald Wingate, 19th May 1884.
20. SAD. 250/1/10. Reginald Wingate to Eddy, 22nd May 1884.
21. SAD. 250/1/23. Eddy to Reginald Wingate, 14th July 1884.
22. Colvile, v.1, p.45

# CHAPTER FOUR
**Egypt and the Sudan (2)**
**The Gordon Relief Expedition**

1. Beresford, v.1, p.256
2. Kochanski, p.161
3. Colvile, v.2, p.8
4. Beresford, v.1, p.269
5. HRO: 21M82, PZ5. Highcliffe Parish Magazine, April 1892.
6. Brit. Lib. Add.MSS.51300, ff.173-176. Eddy to Augusta Gordon, 1st December 1885.
7. Ibid.
8. Colvile, v.2, p.43
9. Beresford
10. Ibid.v.2, p.291
11. Ibid.v.2, p294
12. Cromer, v.2, p.380
13. SA: WhM418. Sir Henry Drummond Wolff to Lord Wharncliffe, 7th November 1885.
14. Cromer, v.2, p.32
15. SA: WhM418. Eddy to Lord Wharncliffe, 7th April 1886.
16. Ibid. Eddy to Lord Wharncliffe, 15th March 1886.

# CHAPTER FIVE
**Marriage and the Army**

1. Wolff, v.2, p.274
2. Stuart Wortley (1), p.234
3. SA: WhM418. Various letters
4. Army Lists
5. *The King's Royal Rifles Corps Chronicle*, 1934, p.178

6. SA: WhM418. Eddy to Lord Wharncliffe, 15th November 1886.
7. Ibid. Lady Waterford to Lord Wharncliffe, 20th October 1887.
8. Ibid. Lady Waterford to Lord Wharncliffe, 20th January 1888.
9. Ibid. Eddy to Lord Wharncliffe, 24th July 1888.
10. Ibid. Lady Montagu of Beaulieu to Lord Wharncliffe, 30th July 1888.
11. Ibid. Mrs James Stuart Wortley to Lord Wharncliffe, 30th July 1888.
12. Ibid. Francis Stuart Wortley to Lord Wharncliffe, 13th August 1888.
13. Brit.Lib Add.MSS.50093, ff.152. Eddy to E.T.H Hutton. 18th May 1889.
14. Hare, v.3, p.465
15. Stuart Wortley (4), p.17
16. *The Times*, 6th February 1891.
17. Memorial tablet, St Mark's Church, Highcliffe.
18. Stuart Wortley (4) and Stuart Wortley (5).
19. Stuart Wortley (1), p.235
20. Stuart Wortley (4), p.45
21. Ibid, p.44
22. Tweedsmuir, p.66
23. SA: WhM418
24. Fitzgerald, p.200
25. Stuart Wortley (5), p.67
26. Ibid.
27. Ibid, p.68
28. Ibid, p.73
29. Stuart Wortley (4), p.30

## CHAPTER SIX
## Egypt and the Sudan (3)
## Omdurman

1. Steevens, p.64
2. Wingate, p.109
3. Who Was Who 1929 - 1940
4. Army List, January 1918, pt.2, p.3072
5. Stuart Wortley (4), p.28
6. Ibid.
7. SAD. 263/1/687. Eddy to Reginald Wingate, 15th September 1897.

8. Pollock, p.117
9. Ibid, p.115
10. Churchill (1), p.174
11. Ibid.
12. Steevens, p.248
13. *The London Gazette*, 30th September 1898
14. Churchill (1), p.185
15. Steevens p.264
16. Ibid, p.291
17. Stuart Wortley (5), p.80
18. *Vanity Fair*, 26th October 1899.

**CHAPTER SEVEN**
**The Boer War (1)**

1. Stuart Wortley (5), p.76
2. Army Lists
3. Stuart Wortley (5), p.77
4. Army List, January 1918, pt.2, p.3072
5. LHCMA. Eddy to Reginald Talbot, 26th December 1899.
6. Treves, p.74
7. Pakenham, p.225
8. Treves, p.75
9. LHCMA. Eddy to Reginald Talbot, 26th December 1899.
10. Treves, p.75
11. Ibid, p.15
12. Ibid, p.18
13. LHMCA. Eddy to Reginald Talbot, 26th December 1899.
14. Churchill (2), p.227
15. Ibid.
16. LCMA. Eddy to Reginald Talbot, 26th December 1899.
17. Pakenham, p.238 et sequ.
18. LCMA. Eddy to Reginald Talbot, 26th December 1899.
19. Pakenham, p.293
20. Stuart Wortley (5), p.80
21. Ibid.
22. Army List, January 1918, pt.2, p.3072
23. LCMA. Eddy to Margaret Talbot, 1st April 1900
24. Ibid.
25. *The London Gazette*, 8th February 1901, p.935
26. Amery, v..3, p.507

27. LCMA. Eddy to Margaret Talbot, 1st April 1900.
28. Amery, v.3, p.507 and Churchill (2), p.399
29. *The London Gazette*, 8th February 1901, p.941.
30. Ibid, p.935
31. Churchill (2), p.408
32. LHMCA. Eddy to Margaret Talbot, 1st April 1900.
33. Army List, January 1918, pt.2, p.3072
34. Ibid.

**CHAPTER EIGHT**
**The Boer War (2)**

1. LHMCA. Eddy to Margaret Talbot, 1st April 1900.
2. Ibid.
3. Ibid.
4. Ibid.
5. Ibid.
6. Pakenham, p.453
7. Army List, January 1918, pt.2, p.3072
8. *The King's Royal Rifle Corps Chronicle*, 1934, p.179
9. Ibid.
10. Pakenham, p.456
11. *The King's Royal Rifle Corps Chronicle*, 1934, p.179

**CHAPTER NINE**
**Home from the War**

1. Stuart Wortley (5), p.78
2. Ibid.
3. Stenton, v.2, p.377
4. Craig, F.W.S p.437
5. Stuart Wortley (5), p.82
6. Ensor, p.268
7. Stuart Wortley (4), p.44
8. Stuart Wortley (5), p.84
9. Visitors' Book
10. Tweedsmuir, p.66
11. Visitors' Book
12. Hare, v.3, p.465
13. Troubridge, p.93
14. Ibid, p.86

15. Rodd, p.298

## CHAPTER TEN
## Paris and the Entente Cordiale

1. Army List, January 1918. Gradation List of Officers of the British Army, Major-Generals.
2. Franklin
3. Gladwin, p.150
4. Ibid, p.151
5. Ibid, p.150
6. Stuart Wortley (4), p.32
7. Ibid, p.36
8. Stuart Wortley (5), p.87
9. Ibid.
10. Ibid.
11. PRO.WO138/29
12. Ibid.
13. Stuart Wortley (4), p.37
14. St. Aubyn, p.321
15. Ibid.
16. Information from the Registrar, The Royal Archives.
17. Magnus, p.311
18. Ibid, p.313
19. Lee, v.2, p.241
20. PRO.WO138/29

## CHAPTER ELEVEN
## Half-Pay

1. SA: WhM418. Lady Waterford to Lord Wharncliffe, December 1886 and 20th October 1887.
2. Visitors' Book
3. *The Daily Telegraph*, 8th July 1930, p.13
4. Who Was Who 1929-1940
5. Stuart Wortley (4), p.42
6. Ibid.
7. Visitors' Book
8. Stuart Wortley (4), p.47
9. Franklin
10. Stuart Wortley (4), p.47

11. Visitors' Book
12. Stuart Wortley (4), p.39
13. Dictionary of National Biography
14. Ensor, p.395
15. *The King's Royal Rifle Corps Chronicle*, 1934, p.178.
16. Army Lists

## CHAPTER TWELVE
### The Kaiser at Highcliffe

1. Bod.Lib. MS.Eng.hist.d.256, fols.1&2
2. Fielding, p.73
3. Ibid.
4. Ibid, p.93
5. Stuart Wortley (5), p.96
6. Stuart Wortley (4), p.48
7. Ibid, p.49
8. HRO: 21M82, PZ8. Highcliffe Parish Magazine, December 1907.
9. Stuart Wortley (4), p.49
10. Ibid.
11. Hole, p.31
12. Bod.Lib.MS.Eng.hist.d.256, fols.19-22
13. Ibid.
14. HRO: 21M82, PZ8. Highcliffe Parish Magazine, January 1908
15. Howard, p.294
16. Ibid.
17. Stuart Wortley (4), p.49

## CHAPTER THIRTEEN
### The *Daily Telegraph* 'Interview'

1. *The Daily Telegraph*, 28th October 1908, p.11
2. Bod.Lib.MS.Eng.hist.d.256, fols.1&2
3. Stuart Wortley (5), p.102
4. Stuart Wortley (4), p.51
5. Bod.Lib.MS.Eng.hist.d.256, fol. 27
6. *The Daily Telegraph*, 8th July 1930, p.13
7. Bod.Lib.MS.Eng.hist.d.256, fols.31-34
8. *The Daily Telegraph*, 8th July 1930, p.13
9. Bod.Lib.MS.Eng.hist.d.256, fols.43-52
10. Ibid, fols.31-34

11. Ibid, fol.31
12. Gooch, p.201 et sequ.
13. Hansard: HC. Deb. 2$^{nd}$ November 1908, vol.195, col.762
14. Palmer, p.134
15. *The Times*, 29$^{th}$ October 1908, p.9
16. Gooch, p. 201
17. Ibid, p.213
18. Bülow, v.3, p.344
19. Ibid.
20. William II, p.116
21. Cowles, p.270
22. Cecil, v.2, p.139
23. Gooch, p.201
24. Bod.Lib.MS.Eng.hist.d.256, fols.58-60
25. Trevelyan, p.464

## CHAPTER FOURTEEN
### Shorncliffe

1. Hart, v.1, p.57
2. Franklin, p.36&79
3. Wolfe
4. Fynemore
5. Stuart Wortley (5), p.112
6. Stuart Wortley (4), p.57
7. Fynemore
8. Stuart Wortley (5), p.104
9. Fynemore
10. Stuart Wortley (5), p.106
11. Ibid, p.112

## CHAPTER FIFTEEN
### The Great War (1)

1. Craig, Gordon A. p.335
2. Stuart Wortley (4), p.65
3. Ibid.
4. Milne, p.4
5. Ibid.
6. PRO.WO.138/29
7. Milne, p.58

8. Gilbert, p.133
9. Middlebrook, p.207
10. Edmonds, p.102
11. Gilbert, p.201
12. Ibid.
13. Edmonds, p.235
14. Ibid, p.384
15. Ibid.
16. Ibid, p.386
17. Edmonds, p.387
18. Ibid.
19. Supplement to *The London Gazette*, 31$^{st}$ December 1915, p.8
20. Graves, p.131
21. Edmonds, p.404
22. PRO.WO.138/29
23. Charteris, p.120
24. Edmonds, p.404
25. Cave, p.41
26. Ibid, p.46
27. Milne, p.73

**CHAPTER SIXTEEN**
**The Great War**
**The First Day of the Somme**

1. Middlebrook, p.74
2. Ibid, p.130
3. Ibid, p.170
4. Dixey, R.N. Unpublished diary.
5. Cannon, p.878
6. Middlebrook, p.263
7. Ibid, p.265
8. Ibid, p.242
9. Ibid, p.267
10. Ibid.
11. PRO. WO.138/29
12. Ibid.
13. Ibid.
14. Ibid.
15. Middlebrook, p.285
16. PRO. WO.138/29

17. Bond, p.41
18. PRO. WO.138/29

## CHAPTER SEVENTEEN
## Ireland

1. PRO. WO.138/29
2. Ibid.
3. Vaughan, p.161
4. Ibid, p.227
5. PRO. WO.138/29
6. Vaughan, p.245

## CHAPTER EIGHTEEN
## The Family in Wartime

1. Hole, p.32
2. Stuart Wortley (4), p.64
3. Stuart Wortley, Rothesay, p.v
4. Stuart Wortley (4), p.66
5. Stuart Wortley (5), p115
6. Stuart Wortley (4), p.66
7. Ibid. p.67
8. Stuart Wortley (5), p118
9. Visitors' Book
10. Stuart Wortley (4), p.66
11. Stuart Wortley (5), p.116
12. Burke's Peerage and Baronetage

## CHAPTER NINETEEN
## Retirement (1)

1. PRO. WO.138/29
2. McPherson, p.408
3. Information from a private source
4. Waterfield, p.187
5. Ibid.
6. Visitors' Book
7. Stuart Wortley (5), p.113
8. Zeldin, v.1, p.427
9. Stuart Wortley (5), p.140

10. Information from Mr R.H.S. Hatton

**CHAPTER TWENTY**
**Retirement (2)**

1. Hare, v.1, p.196
2. Malmesbury, v.1, p.161
3. Troubridge, p.175
4. Waterhouse, p.102
5. Stuart Wortley (4), p.75
6. Pound, p.140
7. Ibid, p.162
8. Ibid.
9. Stuart Wortley (4), p.135
10. *The Times*, 20th March 1934, p.19
11. HRO: 21M82, PZ9. Highcliffe Parish Magazine, May 1934.
12. *The Times*, 20th March, 1934, p.19

# INDEX

Abdurrahman Khan. 11,12
Abingdon, Bettine, Countess of. See Elizabeth Stuart Wortley. Eddy's daughter.
Abingdon, Montagu, 8th Earl of, and 13th Earl of Lindsay. Eddy's son-in-law. 135
Abu Hamed. 43
Abu Klea, The Battle of. 26, 27, **30**
Abyssinia. 41, 43, 136, 138
Afghanistan. 7-12, 31
Afghan War, The First. 7
Afghan War, The Second. 7-12
Agra. 7
Alexandra, Queen of England. 86
Alfonso XII, of Spain. 83
Alfonso XIII, of Spain. 82, 83
Allenby, General Sir Edmund. 117, 119, 122
Amulet. 48, 49
Aosta, Amadeus, 3rd Duke of. 136, 138
Arbuthnot, Forster. 35
Argentine, The. 143
Asquith, Herbert Henry. 126-128
Assioutt (Asyut). 23, 24
Assouan (Aswan). 32
Atbara, The Battle of. 45
Atbara, The Fort. 45
Atbara, The River. 45
Aubers Ridge. 107
Augusta Victoria, Kaiserin. 86, 88
Austria. 105, 130
Aveland, Gilbert, 2nd Baron. 33
Ayub Khan. 11, 12

Baden-Powell, General Sir Robert. Later 1st Baron Baden-Powell. 139
Badger hunt. 102
Baggara tribe. 48
Baker, Valentine. 18
Balesh Khel. 9, 10
Balfour, Arthur. 84
Baring, Sir Evelyn. Later 1st Earl of Cromer. 16, 32, 39, 41
Bastille Day. 77
Bear hunt. 102
Belfast, The Battle of. 68
Belgium. 105
Berber. 43, 45

Beresford, Capt. Lord Charles, RN. Later Admiral and 1st Baron Beresford. 27, 31, 33, 82
Beris. 24
Berlin. 88, 91, 105, 132
Bertie, Montagu. See the 8th Earl of Abingdon.
Bettine Lady Abingdon Collection, Victoria and Albert Museum. 138
Biggarsberg Hills. 66, 67
Black and Tans, The. 129
'Black Week'. 56
Bloomfontein. 13, 64
Boers, The. 12, 50, 52, 54, 56, 58, 60, 62, 63, 66-69, 96
Boer War, The. 50-69, 84, 96, 133
Boodles Club. 82
Borghese, Princess Pauline. 75
Botha, Christiaan. 56
Botha, Louis. 52, 66
Brazil. 143
British Commonwealth. 129
British Expeditionary Force. 129
British Legion, now The Royal British Legion, Highcliffe. 139
British South Africa Company. 50
Brussels. 101
Buchan, John. Later 1st Baron Tweedsmuir. 72
Buchan, Susan, Lady Tweedsmuir. 37
Bulgaria. 143
Buller, General Sir Redvers, VC. 50-52, **53**, 54-63, 64-69
Bülow, Bernhard von. Prince Bülow. 92, 94, 97, 98
Burma. 143
Burnaby, Colonel Frederick. 25, 27
Burne-Jones, Sir Edward, Bart. 37
Burnham, Edward 1st Baron. 93
Bute, James, 1st Earl of. 2
Bute, John, 3rd Earl of. 1, 2, 33
Bute, John, 4th Earl and 1st Marquess of. 1, 2
Bute, John Patrick, 3rd Marquess of. 142
Bute, Mary, Countess of. 1, 2

Cairo. 16, 20, 22, 23, 32, 45
Cambridge, The Duke of. 25
Campbell-Bannerman, Sir Henry. 70, 84
Cape Colony. 12, 50
Cape Town. 50
Cardiff Castle. 142
Carlton, Archibald, Viscount. 135
Carlton, Elfreda, Viscountess. 135

Carpenter, The Reverend Stanley. 84
Carrick-Moore, Mary. 101
Carson, Edward. 127
Cavagnari, Sir Luis. 7
Cavendish Hotel, Jermyn Street. 86
Cayley, Lady Mary. See Mary Stuart Wortley. Eddy's sister.
Cayley, Sir George, Bart. 72
Ceylon. 77, 143
Chamberlain, Joseph. 70
Chatsworth House. 105, 140
Chieveley. 52
Chile. 143
China. 20, 97
Christchurch Priory. 90
Christian of Schleswig-Holstein, Princess. 101
Churchill, Winston. 45, 47, 56, **57**, 63, 71, 134
Clarges Street, Piccadilly. 82, 93
Clery, General Sir Henry. 52
Colenso. 50, 60, 62
Colenso, The Battle of. 52, 54, **55**, 56, 68
Colvile, Henry. Later General Sir Henry. 22, 31
Commons, The House of. 71, 74, 97, 126
Composite Rifles. See the Rifle Reserve Battalion.
Concentration camps. 6
Connaught, The Duke and Duchess of. 39
Conservative Party, The. 70, 126
Constantinople. 32
Cooper, Sir Alfred, FRCS. 86
Cornwall. 37
Corsica. 100
Corunna. 100
Creighton, Lady Caroline. 2
Cromer, Evelyn, 1st Earl of. See Sir Evelyn Baring.
Cronje, Piet. 64
Cuninghame, Margaret. 2
Cuninghame, Sir David, Bart. 2
Curragh, The. 125, 127
Cyprus. 143

*Daily Mail, The.* 48
*Daily Telegraph, The.* 92-99, 102
Derbyshire. 105
Desert Column, The. 25, 27, 29, 31
Devonshire, The Duchess of. 105
Distinguished Service Order. 41

Dongola province. 43
Dongola town. 43
Drakensberg Mountains. 66, 67
Drogheda, Henry, 3rd Marquess of. 4, 6, 125
Drogheda, Mary, Marchioness of. 4, 125
Dublin. 103, 126, 128, 129
Dubski, Count and Countess. 130
Dunn, Jim. 136

Easter Rising, The. 128
Edvina, Madam (Marie Louise Edwardes). 134, 135
Edward, Prince of Wales, and later King Edward VII. 35, **73**, 74, **76**, 79-81, 86
Edward, Prince of Wales, and later King Edward VIII. 142
Egypt. 14-24, 25-32, 39, 41-53, 113, 143
Emily the hen. 60
Ena, Princess. See Princess Victoria Eugenia of Battenberg.
Entente Cordiale, The. 1, 75-81
Eritrea. 41
Erne, John, 1st Earl of. 2
Eton College. 4, 131
Eva (Evelyn Heathcote-Amory-Willoughby). 33
Evans, The Reverend Frederick. 139
Exeter Cathedral. 136

Field Transport. 8, 11
Fifty-Sixth Division. See the London Territorial Division.
First World War. See the Great War 1914-1918.
Firth, J.B. 93
Fishing. 49, 140
Folkestone. 100
*Folkestone Herald, The* 100
Forfarshire. 35
Forty-Sixth Division. See the North Midland Territorial Division.
Fosse 8. 109-111
Fourth Army, The. 117, 122
France. 43, 94, 105, 115, 130, 136
Franz Ferdinand, Archduke, of Austria. 105, 130
French, General Sir John. Later Field Marshal and 1st Earl of Ypres.
                    107, **108**, 109, 113, 124, 129, 134
Frere. 52, 56
Friendlies, The. 43, 45, 48

Gaelic Society of London. 142
Gallwey, Colonel Thomas. 54
Gandamak, The Treaty of. 7

Gatacre, General Sir William. 52, 56
*Gazette, The London.* 47
George III of England. 1
George V of England. 105, 107, 113, 124
German Army. 92, 93, 102
German Navy. 97
Germany. 87-919, 105-124, 127
Ghandi, Mohandas. Mahatma Ghandi. 54
Ginnis, The Battle of. 32
Givenchy. 115
Gladstone, William Ewart. 126
Glastonbury. 146
Gommecourt. 117-120, 125
*Goodbye to All That.* 111
Gordon, Augusta. 29, 43
Gordon, Colonel John. 10
Gordon, General Charles George. 20, **21**, 22, 25-31, 41, 43
Gordon, General Thomas. 9
Gordon Relief Expedition. 1,2, 25-31, 33
Goschen, Sir Edward. 97, 132
Gough, General Hubert. Later General Sir Hubert. 127
Gould, The Reverend Charles. 139
Grant, Captain Allastair Edward. 133
Graves, Robert. 111
Gray, The Reverend Frederick. 84, 139
'Great Game'. 7, 31
Great Oasis. 22, 24
Great War, The. 105-124
Grenfell, General Sir Francis. 32, 41
Grey, Sir Edward. Later 1st Viscount Grey. 86, 98
Grosvenor, Caroline. Formerly Caroline Stuart Wortley. 72
Grosvenor Gallery. 37
Grosvenor, Norman. 72
Grosvenor, Susan. See also Susan Buchan, Lady Tweedsmuir. 72
Gubat. 27, 29, 31
Guildford. 35
Gunboat Flotilla. 43, **44**, 48
Guthrie, James. 35
Guthrie, Lilias. See Lady Rodd.
Guthrie, Murray. 72, 82
Guthrie, Violet. See Violet Stuart Wortley, Eddy's wife.

**Haig**, General Sir Douglas. Later Field Marshal and 1st Earl Haig. 107-113, **114**, 115, 116, 117-124, 125
Haking, General Sir Richard. 113

Haldane, Richard Burdon. 1st Viscount Haldane. 84
Hamilton, General Sir Ian. 132
Hamilton, Lady (Jean). 132
Hants Yeomanry. 131
Harewood, Henry, 3rd Earl of. 2
Harrowby, Dudley, 1st Earl of. 2
Hart, General Fitzroy. 62
Hart's Hill. 62
Heathcote-Amory-Willoughby, Evelyn. See Eva
Helena Victoria, Princess. 101, 132
Henry of Battenburg, Prince. 83
Henry of France, Prince. Later Comte de Paris, Pretender to French Throne. 136
Highcliffe Castle. 33-35, **36**, 37-39, 43, 72, **73**, 74, 82-85, 86-88, **89**, 90, 91, 92, 103, 105, 130, 132, 133, 135, 136, **137**, 138, 139, 142
Highcliffe Parish Church. See St Mark's Church, Highcliffe.
Highcliffe (Village). 83, 84, 86, 90, 139, 142
Highcliffe Working Mens Club, now Highcliffe Sports and Social Club. 139
Hlangwane Hill. 60
Hohenzollern Redoubt. 109-111
*Hohenzollern*, Royal Yacht. 88
Holmfirth, The Parliamentary Constituency of. 70
Home Rule Act of 1912. 126
Hooge. 109
Hunting. 140
Hurn Court. 140

**I**celand. 140
India. 7-12
Inner Temple. 4
Ireland. 4, 103, 125-129, 131, 134
Irish Free State. 129
Irish Republican Brotherhood. 127, 128
Ismailia. 14
Italy. 41, 115, 135

**J**aalin tribe. 47, 48, 58
Jakdu. 25
Jameson Raid. 50
Japan. 90, 97
Joubert, Piet. 66

**'K'** Lady. 32
Kabul. 7-9, 11, 12
Kaiser Wilhelm II. See William II of Germany.
Kandahar. 11, 12

Kedleston Hall. 140
Keppel, Commander Colin, RN. 43
Khaki Election. 70
Khalifa. 32, 41, 45, 47, 48
Khartoum. 20, 22, 25, 27, 29, 43, 45
Khedive of Egypt. 14, 16
Kildare, County. 4, 125
Kildare Rifles. 4, 6
Kimberley. 13, 52, 64
*King Cophetua and the Beggar Maid.* 37
King's Royal Rifle Corps. 7, 63, 64, 72, 143
Kingston Lacy. 90
Kipling, John. 111
Kipling, Rudyard. 111
Kitchener, Horatio Herbert. Later Field Marshal and 1st Earl Kitchener. 23, 40, 41, 45, 47, 48, 64, **65**, 68, 122
Kitiab. 43
Knole. 140
Knollys, Francis, 1st Viscount. 79
Kohat. 8
Koran. 24
Korti. 25
Kurram Valley. 7-11
Kurram Valley Field Force. 7-9
Kushi. 8

Ladysmith. 50, 56, 58, 60, 62-64, 66, 69
Laing's Nek. 67
Langtry, Lillie. 37
Lansdowne, Henry, 5th Marquess of. 56, 79
Lascelles, Lady Susan. See Countess of Wharncliffe.
Laszlo, Philip de. 88
Lawson, Harry. 93
Leighton, Sir Frederic, Bart, PRA. 37
Leslie, Sir John and Lady Constance. 72
Leslie, Olive. 72
Lewis, Rosa. 86, 87
Liberal Party, The. 70, 126
Liddell Hart, Sir Basil. 100
Light Brigade. 100
Lille. 107
Lisbon. 79
Lloyd George, David. 70, 101, 102, 128, 133, 134
*London Gazette, The.* 47
London Territorial Division (56th). 117, 119, 120

Loos, The Battle of. 109, 113, 115
Loraine, Lady (Louise). See Louise Stuart Wortley. Eddy's daughter. 135, 143
Loraine, Sir Percy, Bart. Eddy's son-in-law. 135, 143
Lords, The House of. 126
Loubet, Emile. President of the French Republic. 79-81
Lowe, General Drury. 16
Lyttelton, General Neville. Later General Sir Neville. 60, 64, 66, 103
Lyttelton, Katherine. See Katherine Stuart Wortley.

**Mac**Donald, General Sir Hector. 77
Mackenzie, Sir George, of Rosehaugh. 2
Mafeking. 52, 67
Maffey, Sir John. 143
Mahdi. 20, 22, 27, 29, 31, 32
Mahdists. 41, 43, 45, 47, 48
Maiwand, The Battle of. 11, 12
Malmesbury, James. 1st Earl of. 140
Malta. 39
Marchesi, Madame Mathilde. 83
Maria Christina, Queen of Spain. 83
Marseilles. 113
Martin, Maria Elizabeth. See Maria Stuart Wortley. Eddy's mother.
Martin, William Benet. Eddy's grandfather. 4
Mary, Queen of England. **137**, 138
Maxwell, General Sir John. 128
Melba, Dame Nellie. (Mitchell, Helen Porter) 83, 101, 138
Melbourne. 83
Metemmeh. 25, 27, 29, 43, 45
Methuen, General Lord. 52, 56
Middlebrook, Martin. 120-124
Millais, Alice. 66
Millais, Effie. 37
Millais, Sir John, Bart, RA. 66
Milner, Alfred, 1st Viscount. 133
Monasterevin. 4
Monson, Lady (Eleanor). 75
Monson, Sir Edmund, Bart. 75, 79, 81
Montagu of Beaulieu, Cicely, Lady. 35, 72
Montagu of Beaulieu, Henry, 1st Baron. 74
Montagu of Beaulieu, John, 2nd Baron. **73**, 74, 140
Montagu-Stuart-Wortley-Mackenzie, Archibald. See the Viscount Carlton.
Montagu-Stuart-Wortley-Mackenzie, Edward. See 3rd Baron and 1st Earl of
 Wharncliffe
Montagu-Stuart-Wortley-Mackenzie, Francis (Frank). See 2nd Earl of
 Wharncliffe

Monte Cristo Hill. 60
Moore Abbey. 4
Moore, General Sir John. 100, 101
*Morning Post, The.* 56
Morocco. 94, 143
Mountstuart, John, Viscount. Later 4th Earl and 1st Marquess of Bute. 1, 2
Mudeford. 90
Mull, The Island of. 82
Muriel. 32
Mussolini, Benito. 136
Mussoorie. 8

**N**aples. 50, 102
Natal. 12, 52, 54, 56, 60, 66
Natal Field Force. 50
Neuve Chapelle, The Battle of. 107, 109, 115
New Forest. 140
New York. 131
Ney, Michel, Marshal. 138
Nile, The River. 25-32, 43, 45, 47
Normanton, The Earls of. 140
North Midland Territorial Division (46th). 105-116, 117-124, 131
Nostell Priory. 140

**O**ldham, The Parliamentary Constituency of. 71
Omdurman. 29, 41-48
Omdurman, The Battle of. 1, **46**, 47, 48, 58, 143
Orange Free State. 12, 51, 52, 64, 66, 67
Orange River Colony. See Orange Free State.
Osborne House. 82
Ottoman Empire. 14, 29, 41-48
Oxford. 101, 131

**P**aardeberg, The Battle of. 64
Palace House, Beaulieu. 72, 140
Palmerston, Henry, 3rd Viscount. 66
Papillon Soldiers' Home. 102
Parliament Act of 1911. 126
Paris. 75-81, 82, 83, 94, 130, 138
Paris, The Comte de. See Prince Henry of France.
Pearse, Patrick. 128
Peel, Sir Robert. 2
Pendant. See amulet.
Peninsular War. 100, 140
Peshawar. 8

Pieters Hill. 62, 63
Polo. 7, 49
Portland Place. 35
Portugal. 143
Potgieters. 58
Potgieter's Drift. 58
Poynter, Sir Edward, Bart, RA. 37
Pozieres. **123**
Pretoria. 56, 66-68
Primo de Rivera, José Antonio. 83
Punchestown Races. 103

**R**awalpindi. 8
Rawlinson, General Sir Henry. 117
Redmond, John. 127
Reform Bill of 1832. 2
Reichstag, The. 97
Rhodes, Cecil. 50
Rifle Reserve Battalion. 60, 62, 63
River Column, The. 25, 27, 29, 31
Roberts, General Sir Frederick, VC. Later Field Marshal & 1$^{st}$ Earl Roberts, VC.
8, 9, 11, 56, **59**, 64, 66-69, 97
Roberts, Lieutenant Frederick, VC. 46, 56
Rodd, Lady (Lilias). 35, 39, 91, 102
Rodd, Sir (James) Rennell. 35, 39, 74, 102, 135, 143
Rome. 79, 83, 102, 135
Romney, George. 142
Rothschild, Baron Ferdinand de. 140
Royal Flying Corps. 113, 131
Royal Green Jackets Museum, Winchester. 48
Royal Navy. 97
Royal Victorian Order. 81
Russell, General Baker. Later Sir Baker. 16, 18
Russia. 7, 31, 94, 115
Ryder, Lady Georgiana. 2

*Safieh*, Steamer. 31
Sailing. 49
St. Aubyn, Giles. 79
St. John of Jerusalem, The Order of. 39
St. Mark's Church, Highcliffe. 84, 90, 138, 139, 143
St. Petersburg. 96
St. Peter's Church, Eaton Square. 35
Salisbury Cathedral. 136
Salisbury, Robert, 3$^{rd}$ Marquess of. 70

Sandgate. 100
Sandhurst, Royal Military College. 6
Sarajevo. 105, 130
Scarborough. 4
Schoen, William von. 94
Scotland. 1, 2, 37, 125
Scott Montagu, The Honourable John. See 2nd Baron Montagu of Beaulieu.
Scout Movement. 139
Seely, Colonel John. 127
Selfridge, Gordon. 142
Selimeh (Selima). 22, 24
Serbia. 105
Shaftesbury, The Earl and Countess of. 138
Sheffield. 1
Shendi. 43
Shir Ali. 7
Shooting. 49, 140
Shorncliffe Camp. 100-104
Signals. 8, 9
Simla. 8, 12
Sinn Fein. 126, 128, 129
Sixty Fifth (2nd Lowland) Territorial Division. 125
Smith-Dorrien, General Sir Horace. 107
Snow, General Sir Thomas. 119-124, 125, 134
Somerley House. 140
Somme, The. 107, 115, 129
Somme, The Battle of the. 1, **112**, **116**, 117, **118**, 119, 120, **121**, 122-124
South Africa. 12, 50, **51**, 52-69, 70-72, 133, 139
South Street, Grosvenor Square. 4
Soveral, Luis, Marquis de. **78**, 79, 80
Spain. 83
Spion Kop. 58, 60
Spion Kop, The Battle of. 58
'Spy'. 1, **3**, 6
Staff College, Camberley. 35, 39
Steevens, George. 48
Stephenson, General Sir Frederick. 32
Stewart, General Sir Herbert. 25, 27, **28**
Stirling, Admiral Sir James. 35
Stirling, Lady (Elinor). 35
Stratford House. 72
Stretcher Bearers, The Voluntary Corps of. 52
Stuart, Charles. See 1st Baron Stuart de Rothesay.
Stuart de Rothesay, Charles, 1st Baron. 33, 37, 75, 83, 100, 138, 140, 142, 143
Stuart, The Honourable James Archibald. Later Stuart-Wortley-Mackenzie. 2

Stuart, The Honourable Lady (Louisa). 142
Stuart, John. See 3rd Earl of Bute.
Stuart, John. See the Viscount Mountstart.
Stuart Mackenzie, James. 2
Stuart of Wortley, Charles, 1st Baron. 66
Stuart Wortley, Archibald. 66, 139
Stuart Wortley, Bettine (Elizabeth). Eddy's daughter. Became Countess of Abingdon. 40, 91, 101, 102, 130, 131, 133, 135
Stuart Wortley, General The Honourable Sir (Alan) Richard. Eddy's brother. 4, 72, 135
Stuart Wortley, The Honourable Francis. Eddy's father. 2, 4, 33, 35
Stuart Wortley, The Honourable James. 64
Stuart Wortley, The Honourable Ralph. Eddy's brother. 4, 72, 135, 136
Stuart Wortley, Jim. 135
Stuart Wortley, Katherine. 64, 103
Stuart Wortley, Lady (Maud). 135
Stuart Wortley, Louise. Eddy's daughter. Became Lady Loraine. 40, 91, 101, 102, 103, 133, 135, 143
Stuart Wortley, Maria. The Honourable Mrs Francis. Eddy's mother. 4, 8, 9, 12, 23, 35, 71
Stuart Wortley, Marie Louise. See Madam Edvina.
Stuart Wortley, Marjorie. 135
Stuart Wortley, Mary or May. Later Lady Mary Cayley. Eddy's sister. 4, 72
Stuart Wortley, Rothesay. Eddy's son. 40, 91, 101-103, 131, 135
Stuart Wortley, Violet. The Honourable Mrs Edward. Eddy's wife. 35, 37, 39, 43, 50, 58, 60, 70-72, 77, 79-83, 91, 92, 101, 102, 105, 130-133, 135, 136, **137**, 138, 140, **141**, 142-144
Stuart-Wortley-Mackenzie, Edward. Later Montagu-Stuart-Wortley-Mackenzie. See 3rd Baron and 1st Earl of Wharncliffe.
Stuart-Wortley-Mackenzie, James Archibald. See 1st Baron Wharncliffe.
Stuart-Wortley-Mackenzie, John. See 2nd Baron Wharncliffe, Eddy's grandfather.
Sturgis, Lady Rachel. 135
Sturgis, Sir Mark. 135
Sudan. 14-24, 25, **26**, 27-32, 41-53, 143
Suez Canal. 14

Talbot, Margaret. Formerly Margaret Stuart Wortley, later Lady Talbot. 60, 63, 64, 66, 72
Talisman. See amulet.
Tate Britain. 37
Tehran. 135
Tel-el-Kebir, The Battle of. 14, 16, **17**
Thal. 8
Third Army, The. 117, 119, 122
*Times, The*. 69, 97, 143

Transvaal. 12, 13, 50, 52, 66-68
Trevelyan, George Macaulay. 99
Treves, Frederick, FRCS. Later Sir Frederick. 52, 54
Trickhardt's Drift. 58
Tugela Heights, The Battle of. 60, **61**, 62, 64
Tugela River. 52, 62
Turf Club, The. 82, 125
Turkey. 14, 32, 33
Tyke the dog. 8
Tytler, General John, VC. 10

Uitlanders. 50
Ulster. 126, 127
Unionists. 126, 127

Vaal Krantz. 60
Vaal Krantz, The Battle of. 60
*Vanity Fair*. 1, **3**, 6, 48
Verdun. 115, 117
Vesey, Constance. 20, 32
Victor Emmanuel III of Italy. 136
Victoria and Albert Museum. 138
Victoria Eugenia of Battenberg, Princess. 83
Victoria, Queen of England. 39, 71, 83, 97, 101, 132
Vimy Ridge. 115, 117

Waddesdon Manor. 140, 142
Wad Hamed. 45
Wadi Halfa. 25, 32, 43
War Office. 14, 105, 122, 125
Warren, General Sir Charles. 58
Waterford, Louisa, Marchioness of. 33, **34**, 35, 72, 75, 83, 142
'Waverers'. 2
Welbeck. 140
Wellington, Arthur, 1st Duke of. 140
Wells Cathedral. 136
Western Australia. 35
Western Desert.22
Western Front, The. **106**, 107, **112**, 115
Wharncliffe Chase. 1
Wharncliffe, Edward, 3rd Baron and 1st Earl of. Eddy's uncle. 2, 4, 6, 14, 18, 20, 32, 33, 35, 37, **38**, 71, 72
Wharncliffe, Francis (Frank), 2nd Earl of. Eddy's brother. 2, 4, 6, 71
Wharncliffe House, Curzon Street. 6, 37, 72
Wharncliffe, James Archibald. 1st Baron. 2, 64

Wharncliffe, John, 2nd Baron. Eddy's grandfather. 2
Wharncliffe Lodge. 1
Wharncliffe, Susan, Countess of. 2, 6, 18, 37
White, General Sir George. 50, 56, 63, 69
William II of Germany. 1, 85, 86, **87**, 88, **89**, 90-99
William IV of England. 37
Wilson, Colonel Sir Charles. 25, 27, 31
Wilson, General Henry. Later Field Marshal Sir Henry. 127
Wilson, Henry, MP. 70
Winchester Cathedral. 136
Wingate, Reginald. Later General Sir Reginald. 23, 41, 43, 45
Witwatersrand. 13
Wolfe, Charles. 100
Wolff, Sir Henry Drummond. 32, 33
Wolseley, General Sir Garnet. Later Field Marshal and 1st Viscount Wolseley. 14, 15, 25-31
Wood, General Sir Evelyn, VC. 18, **19**, 22, 32
Wood, Lieutenant C.M.A. 47
Worsborough Hall. 4
'Wortley Avenue'. 115
Wortley Hall. 1, **5**, 37, 72
Wortley Montagu, Edward. 1
Wortley Montagu, Mary. 1

Yakub Khan. 7, 11
Yapp, Sir Arthur. 132
Yarmouth, Francis, Earl of. Later 3rd Marquess of Hertford. 138
Yorkshire. 1, 37, 70
Young, Captain Reginald. **118**
Young Men's Christian Association. 131, 132
Ypres Salient. 107

Zaimukht tribe. 9, 10
Zawo. 10